MAKING NOTHING

All the authors in this collection agree that being committed to a religious form of words and practices is not simply 'the conscious occupation of the mind praying' (Eliot's phrase) but a set of habits that allows, and eventually demands, space in us. The authors write, poetry and prose alike, to demonstrate that these habits bring something to life, make space for others. So this is a book about a coming to life and a coming to stillness, together and inseparable; a serious and joyful gift, for which this reader is deeply grateful.

From the Foreword by Rowan Williams,
Master of Magdalene College Cambridge

This thoughtful, generative interaction of poets is a welcome entry into the current struggle for and with faith among us. It is clear that the long-standing prose attempts of memo and proposition produce certitude and absolutism, but not much in the way of energy or courage or wisdom. These poets are knowing in thick ways, elusive enough to invite us to move with them, and critical in ways to hint at fresh connections. In all, a welcome resource.

Walter Brueggemann, Professor Emeritus,
Columbia Theological Seminary, USA

Is religious poetry a brand of 'minor poetry' as TS Eliot feared? Or can it, through forging new metaphors and enlivening old ones, provide a new music for this age of fragile faith and doubt? These are vital questions for Christianity, a faith founded on the poetry of the Bible, and this book by five leading poet-theologians is a timely and challenging contribution to the debate.

Michael Symmons Roberts, Professor of Poetry,
Manchester Metropolitan University, UK

Making Nothing Happen is a conversation between five poet-theologians broadly within the Christian tradition – Nicola Slee, Ruth Shelton, Mark Pryce, Eleanor Nesbitt and Gavin D'Costa. Together they form *The Diviners*.

Each poet offers an illuminating reflection on how they understand the relation between poetry and faith, rooting their reflections in their own writing, and illustrating discussion with a selection of their own poems. The poets open up issues for deeper exploration and reflection, including: the nature of creativity and the distinction between divine and human creation; the creative process as exploration, epiphany and revelation; the forging of identity through writing; ways in which the arts reflect, challenge and dialogue with faith, and faith can inform and challenge the arts; power and voice in poetry and faith; and ways in which race, gender and culture interact with and shape poetic and theological discourse.

This book will be of interest to poets and theologians, to all interested in the connections between literature and faith, to those seeking inspiration for preaching, liturgy and pastoral care, and to those committed to the practice and nurturing of a contemplative attitude to life in which profound attention and respect are offered to words and to the creative Word at work.

Making Nothing Happen
Five Poets Explore Faith and Spirituality

GAVIN D'COSTA
University of Bristol, UK

ELEANOR NESBITT
University of Warwick, UK

MARK PRYCE
Diocese of Birmingham, UK

RUTH SHELTON
Nottingham, UK

NICOLA SLEE
Queen's Foundation, Birmingham, UK

ASHGATE

Published by
Ashgate Publishing Limited
Wey Court East
Union Road
Farnham
Surrey, GU9 7PT
England

Ashgate Publishing Company
110 Cherry Street
Suite 3-1
Burlington, VT 05401-3818
USA

www.ashgate.com

British Library Cataloguing in Publication Data
A catalogue record for this book is available from the British Library

The Library of Congress has cataloged the printed edition as follows:
LoC data has been applied for

ISBN 9781409455172 (hbk)
ISBN 9781409455158 (pbk)
ISBN 9781409455165 (ebk – PDF)
ISBN 9781472406941 (ebk – ePUB)

Printed in the United Kingdom by Henry Ling Limited,
at the Dorset Press, Dorchester, DT1 1HD

Contents

Notes on Contributors

Gavin D'Costa started writing poetry while at school and has continued since. He has written one unpublished novel and dabbles with oil painting. He taught a religion and literature degree course for some years. He is a Roman Catholic married to a Quaker and has two teenage children. He is consultant to the English and Welsh Bishops and the Vatican and also the Anglican Church on matters of theology and religious pluralism. Gavin is Professor of Catholic Theology at the University of Bristol. His publications include *Vatican II: Interpreting the Roman Catholic View on Other Religions* (Oxford University Press, 2014); *Christianity and World Religions. Disputed Questions in the Theology of Religions* (Blackwell, 2009); *Theology in the Public Square* (Blackwell, 2005); *Sexing the Trinity* (SCM, 2000) and *The Trinity and the Meeting of Religions* (T & T Clark, 2000).

Eleanor Nesbitt has read and written poetry since her primary school days. When religious labels are called for she sometimes explains that she is a Quaker, of Anglican background, that Sikh tradition has left a deep imprint and that she is part of a Hindu family. Her poems have appeared as *Turn But a Stone* (Hilton House, 1999) and in *Gemini Four* (OnlyConnect, 2011), in *Of Faith and Friendship: In Memory of David Bowen* (Bradford College, 2000) and *Bare Feet and Buttercups: Resources for Ordinary Time* (Wild Goose Publications, 2008). Eleanor is Professor Emeritus (Religions and Education) at the University of Warwick. Her publications include *Sikhism: A Very Short Introduction* (Oxford University Press, 2005); *Intercultural Education: Ethnographic and Religious Approaches* (Sussex Academic Press, 2004); and *Interfaith Pilgrims* (Quaker Books, 2003). Co-authored volumes include (with Robert Jackson) *Hindu Children in Britain* (Trentham, 1993); (with Gopinder Kaur) *Guru Nanak* (Bayeux Arts, 1999) and (with Kailash Puri) *Pool of Life: The Autobiography of a Punjabi Agony Aunt* (Sussex Academic Press, 2013).

Mark Pryce grew up in Oswestry, in the Welsh Marches, where his poetic imagination was shaped by the liturgy and music of the Anglican choral tradition and the remote beauty of the Shropshire-Montgomeryshire hills. He read English at the University of Sussex and trained for ordained ministry in the Church of England at Westcott House, Cambridge. He has served as a University Chaplain and inner-city parish priest. His poetry explores themes in Christian spirituality and worship, rooted in his work as a pastor, teacher and practical theologian. In *Finding a Voice* (SCM, 1996) Mark offers poetry as one source for reimagining masculinity. His *Literary Companion to the Lectionary* (SPCK/Fortress, 2001) and *Literary Companion for Festivals* (SPCK/Fortress, 2003) draw on poetry as a resource for personal devotion and public worship. More recently Mark has collaborated with theologians Paula Gooder and James Woodward in poetic interpretations of the four Gospels (SPCK, 2011, 2012, 2013, forthcoming 2014). Mark is Bishop's Adviser for Clergy Continuing Ministerial Education in Birmingham Diocese and an Honorary Canon of Birmingham Cathedral.

Ruth Shelton is a poet and theologian presently working as Chief Executive at Emmanuel House in Nottingham, a Centre for homeless, vulnerably housed and marginalised people. She has taught Pastoral Theology at Campion House, Osterley and at the University of Nottingham (EMMTC) and was Director of Social Responsibility for the Diocese of Southwell and Nottingham between 1991 and 1998. A Roman Catholic, she has worked in a wide variety of settings including as Reader-in-Residence in three Leicestershire Prisons, and Poet-in-Residence at the then Shepherd School in Nottingham (now Oak Field School) for students with Special Educational Needs. In 2004 she worked in partnership with Barnardos, supporting sexually exploited young women in the writing of diary material for an exhibition at The Women's Library in Whitechapel. (As Ruth Hobson) she has regularly published poems over many years in magazines including *Magma*, *Ambit*, *Poetry London*, *Delinquent* and *London Magazine*.

Nicola Slee grew up near the wild coast of North Devon, a landscape that continues to inform her writing and sense of self. She has written poetry since childhood and had poems published in many anthologies and journals. A lay Anglican, she is active in a number of groups and networks campaigning for the full inclusion of women and sexual minorities in the churches. She is Research Fellow at the Queen's Foundation for Ecumenical Theological Education, Birmingham (half-time) and a freelance writer, speaker and consultant. Her publications include *Seeking the Risen Christa* (SPCK, 2011); *The Book of Mary* (SPCK, 2007); *Women's Faith Development: Patterns and Processes* (Ashgate, 2004); *Praying Like a Woman* (SPCK, 2004) and *Faith and Feminism: An Introduction to Christian Feminist Theology* (DLT, 2003). Co-edited texts include *Presiding Like a Woman* (co-edited with Stephen Burns; SPCK, 2010) and *The Edge of God: New Liturgical Texts and Contexts in Conversation* (co-edited with Michael Jagessar and Stephen Burns; Epworth Press, 2008).

Foreword

By Rowan Williams, Master of Magdalene College Cambridge,
and Former Archbishop of Canterbury

Poetry is always an act of faith. People write poetry in the eccentric confidence that, by allowing 'normal' speech to be pressed and manipulated out of shape by some perception or obsession or unlikely recognition, they will discover something they didn't know they knew. Poetry is among many other things a way of finding out what's in your mind – which will include finding a great deal you didn't consciously put there. When poetry is written out of a mind informed by specifically religious faith, you might well want to say that this includes a lot you didn't even *unconsciously* put there – echoes of Simone Weil's great aphorism that faith has to do with 'the connections we cannot make'. The poetic discovery is a discovery of connectedness that has been stumbled across, not laboriously engineered – through assonance and puns and sometimes absurd associations (not unlike dreaming). The hard work of poetry is not putting together coherent schemes but feeling your way through words, weighing and trying them, as if they were material for a drystone wall (a metaphor that dawned on me in a poem I wrote over 30 years ago), finding the shape that is suggesting itself. And that happens when some sorts of guard are down, perhaps when 'nothing is happening'.

The introduction underlines the double sense of 'making nothing happen'. Poems don't change the outside world (do they? depends what sort of change, I suppose), but they do change the landscape of language so that space appears. And the space that a poem creates for a reader or speaker is a sort of mirror of the space in the poet that allows all this work to be done, the 'nothing' that happens in the process of making a poem. The faith that out of this nothingness there is a shared discovery and a new space cleared is actually just as ambitious an act as any commitment to doctrine; indeed, we understand a lot better what a commitment to religious doctrine might be if we are able to sense that the words of our belief systems are supposed to 'make nothing happen' – to bring us to a space of discovery and recognition. All the authors in this collection would agree, I think, that being committed to a religious form of words and practices is not simply 'the conscious occupation of the mind praying' (Eliot's phrase), but a set of habits that allows – and eventually demands – space in us. They write – poetry and prose alike – to demonstrate that these habits bring something to life, make space for others. So this is a book about a coming to life and a coming to stillness, together and inseparable; a serious and joyful gift, for which this reader is deeply grateful.

Acknowledgements

We are grateful to Sarah Lloyd at Ashgate for her enthusiasm for this project and for her support throughout, and to a variety of colleagues, partners and friends who have read versions of our essays and poems and commented on them. Particular thanks go to Rowan Williams for writing the Foreword and for his continuing membership of the group, *in absentia*.

Acknowledgements of Copyright

The following individuals and publishing houses have kindly given us permission to quote copyright material. We acknowledge our gratitude to each of them.

Angela Topping for permission to quote from 'How to Capture a Poem', Ray Muna for permission to quote from her haiku in Dear (2012) and Margaret Crompton for permission to quote from 'Sunday Birding' in Dear (2012). Sibyl Ruth for allowing the quotation from 'A Song of Jean' (2008), Gwyneth Lewis for permission to quote from 'How to knit a poem' and Wendy Cope for permission to quote from 'An Argument with Wordsworth' (1992). *Delinquent* for permission to reprint 'Swedenborg's Drains' by Ruth Shelton.

Artemispoetry for permission to reprint 'Envoys' by Nicola Slee; Bloodaxe Books for permission to quote from R.S. Thomas, *Collected Later Poems: 1988– 2000* (Bloodaxe Books, 2004); Church in Wales Publications for permission to reprint 'Litter stick' by Euros Bowen; Faber for permission to quote from David Jones, *The Sleeping Lord and Other Fragments* (London: Faber and Faber 1974) and from Adam Zagajewski, *Mysticism for Beginners* (New York: Farrar Straus Giroux, 1999); HarperCollins for permission to quote from Allen Ginsberg, *Collected Poems 1947–1980* (New York: Harper and Row, 1984); SCM for permission to reprint poems by Mark Pryce from *Finding a Voice: Women and Men in the Community of the Church* (SCM, 1996); SPCK for permission to reprint poems by Mark in his *Literary Companion to the Lectionary* (SPCK/Fortress 2001) and *Literary Companion for Festivals* (SPCK/Fortress 2003) as well as from *Journeying with Mark, Journeying with Luke* and *Journeying with Matthew* (SPCK, 2011, 2012, 2013); SPCK also for permission to use poems by Nicola Slee in *Praying Like a Woman* (SPCK, 2004), *The Book of Mary* (SPCK, 2007), *Presiding Like a Woman* (SPCK, 2010) and *Seeking the Risen Christa* (SPCK, 2011).

Introduction

W.H. Auden famously said, 'poetry makes nothing happen' (2007: 246). Like the best aphorisms, this one makes an immediate impact and yet also repays deeper reflection. We might initially regard it as a wholly negative statement which cuts poetry down to size and resists grandiose claims for what literature can do in a life, a culture or a society. Read in this way, we might want to query, qualify or refute Auden's claim. Yet it is possible to read the statement otherwise, as a more positive, albeit paradoxical affirmation. What if poetry really *does* do something, at least to those who read it, and what if that something is, paradoxically, 'nothing'? Read in this way, Auden's aphorism might then be gesturing towards poetry's potential to open up creative, empty space, a space which invites the harried reader, heckled by all kinds of other discourse – each of which seeks to accomplish some particular end – into a void in which all utilitarian ends are refused and language is celebrated and experienced in all its apophatic, contemplative glory. Poetry is then distinguished from every other form of language which is concerned with specific and identifiable aims, and is the speech form that points us most inexorably to the mystery and freedom of the creative Word, source of all being and knowing.

In this collection of essays and poems by five poets who are also persons of Christian faith (generously understood), and theologians (of differing kinds), we seek to explore and reflect on the mysterious, graced potential of poetry to open up a space that some may describe as sacred, spiritual or religious, although ultimately defying precise categorisation. While many secular poets would roundly refute such a claim, there are others for whom poetry, in its forms as much as its content, is close to the language and purposes of prayer, incantation, ritual and liturgy and, by its rhythms, silences, patterns and sounds, as well as by its qualitative attention to concretion, particularity, ordinariness and otherness, can invoke a profoundly contemplative, morally serious regard for the world.

As far as we have been able to discover, there are no strictly comparable texts to what we intend and offer in this collection. There are a number of anthologies of Christian/religious/spiritual poetry (including Batchelor, 1995; Atwan, Dardess and Rosenthal, 1998; Atwan and Wieder, 2000; Astley and Robertson-Pearce, 2007) but these texts contain little prose and are trying to do something very different from what we intend. Then there are a number of prose texts that address the relation between poetry and faith (for example, Bowker, 1993; Countryman, 1999; Edwards, 2005; Griffiths, 2005; Guite, 2012), but again these represent a different genre from what we are attempting, insofar as they are solo-authored texts exploring poetry and faith in a more systematic, discursive fashion, and they tend to look to a classic tradition of religious poetry rather than being focused on contemporary verse. Then again, there are more popular books aimed at a broader spirituality audience (such as Housden, 2002, 2003, 2007; Morley, 2011). These texts do combine poems and prose discussion, with reflective comments offered on a selection of poems, but they too tend to be single-authored and less clearly rooted in one particular religious tradition. If there is anything that seeks to do what we are doing in this book, it is perhaps the journal *Scintilla*, published since 1997 by the Usk Valley Vaughan Association, in honour of, and continuing the tradition of, the poet-physician Henry Vaughan and his priest-alchemist twin brother, Thomas. This beautifully produced annual journal brings together literary scholarship, theological reflection and creative writing, combining new poetry with essays by living poets and critical, historical and theological articles, particularly but not exclusively on the Vaughans. We would like to think that our book stands in the same kind of tradition as this unique journal – and encourage readers who do not know of the journal to find it, read it and support it. We might also mention a Flarestack pamphlet which brings together a range of contemporary poets to reflect on the question, *Is a religious poem possible in the early 21st century?* (Hart, 2004) Each of the poets offers very brief reflections alongside one or two poems. Again, our book is in the same spirit and tradition as that pamphlet, but what we offer is a more extended treatment from out of the life of one particular group.

In our contributions to the present volume we all share something of our own histories and narratives of how we came to be interested in – or perhaps better, grasped by – the connections between poetry and faith, and how we understand poetry through the lens of our own particular faith traditions and perspectives.

Although these narratives are offered as individual pieces which might stand on their own, their context in the life of the Diviners group to which we all belong significantly shapes and informs each piece, and this book would not have come into being without the history of the group.

We have been meeting as a group for some twelve years. Scattered around the Midlands (located respectively in Bristol, Birmingham, Coventry and Nottingham), we meet about three times a year, usually for a day, to share food and news, to read recent work and to respond to and critique each other's writing. The group emerged out of conversations between various members, each of whom already knew at least one of the others. Rowan Williams was, for a short period, a member of the group before a new 'day job' as Archbishop of Canterbury precluded further involvement. We are grateful for his willingness to contribute a foreword and thus be present in this collaborative enterprise. Mark has joined the group most recently. The group is forged out of strong connecting threads, both personal and professional, as well as encompassing creative differences. Each of us is a practising member of a Christian faith tradition: two Roman Catholic (Gavin and Ruth), two Anglicans (Nicola and Mark) and one Quaker (Eleanor). (We are mindful of the fact that, in the UK, Quakers debate whether, and in what ways, they should individually or collectively espouse the historically complex label 'Christian'.)

Each of us would regard ourselves as theologians or religious studies practitioners, though working in diverse contexts and at different levels. Gavin and Eleanor are firmly rooted in the academy, with professorial posts in British universities – Gavin's in Catholic Theology, Eleanor's, as an ethnographer, in Religions and Education; Mark supports clergy learning and ministerial development in a diocesan post; Nicola's context in a church-sponsored theological institution which runs university-validated programmes combines both church and academy; and Ruth has worked in a wide variety of church, educational and social justice contexts, reflecting a more grassroots perspective of the intersections between church, society and education. While each is more or less firmly rooted in Christian tradition, we also each look to other sources and traditions for inspiration and dialogue: Eleanor has for four decades been engaged academically and personally with other – notably Hindu and Sikh – faith communities; Gavin has written on and been involved with members of the Jewish, Muslim, Hindu and Buddhist traditions, from a Catholic standpoint; Mark looks to the ways in which poetry and creative writing are used in fields of professional development beyond the churches, and he also has a particular interest in gender studies and pastoral theology as these relate to men and masculinities; Nicola has a particular commitment to feminism and gender studies, as well as to the intersection between poetry and liturgy; and Ruth has wide-ranging commitments to art, politics and social justice.

In 2006 we were invited to organise and lead a Radio 4 Sunday Morning Service, and worked with the producer, Claire Campbell-Smith, and David Ogden's talented choral group based in Bristol, to create a service of words and music which explored the connections between faith and poetry. It was at that point that we gave ourselves a name, happening upon 'the Diviners' after a great deal of banter. The name evokes the divine as well as being suggestive of our shared conviction that poetry itself may be a form of divination, a means of searching for the sacred, but also the means whereby we ourselves are searched out and our lives become the sacred ground in which the holy is discerned. Like water divining, poetry is a quest for the sources of life and renewal that the poet believes to be deeply embedded in the ground of his or her existence, yet which often remain elusive, below the obvious surface of things, necessitating exploration in uncharted territory. Sometimes the poet and the poem strike lucky, the rock is struck, waters gush forth. Sometimes the poet returns thirsty and empty, the words refuse to come or, when they do, remain inert, obfuscating, dry. Poetry, no less than water divining, requires patience, practice, repetition, failure and return, as one works the terrain over and over, paying close attention to cartography but knowing when the maps have to be abandoned in pursuit of the spring of life.

The task that we set ourselves in the creation of this text was to each select poems which we wished to represent our body of work. These would be poems that express from many perspectives our individual engagement with divinity, poems which, icon-like, allow the reader or listener to go beyond or through the surface. The further challenge was to set out in prose our understanding and experience of faith and poetry, angel and muse, wonder and word. In the process we would be sharing our life-stories and providing contextual comment on our selected poems. After sharing our drafts we met to reflect further and to plan the integration of our contributions.

At this point the distinctive voices and the resonances between them rang out. Gavin provides autobiographical and theological reflections about poetry and divine creativity and of how we participate in that creativity when we read and write poems. Nicola's essay speaks of feminist theology and the quest for authenticity and integration within a poetic discourse that is also a form of theology. Eleanor's contribution – as an ethnographer who is part of a religiously plural family – springs from experience of diversity as 'inter-spirituality', an interior dialogue. The spirituality born of engagement with issues of poverty and justice infuses Ruth's work. Mark's reflection on the formation and identity of a Christian poet draws on the concerns of Practical Theology and spirituality which underlie his writing.

Every reader will detect different resonances between our voices. In terms of subject, one convergence is Death Row (Gavin and Ruth), another is urban spaces (Ruth and Eleanor), another is sexuality and gendered approaches to faith (Nicola, Ruth and Mark). Gavin and Eleanor suggest experiences of diversity which contrast as much as they converge – Gavin with a family history of conversion from Hindu to Catholic and of migration from India, via Africa, to England; Eleanor with a trajectory that took her from her English Protestant background to India and then (in England) into a Hindu family. The sharing of childhoods and upbringing enables us, and the reader, to situate our poetry with more awareness. Worship – as response to 'nature', as liturgical form, as the experience of the Mass or Meeting for Worship – replenishes and evokes some, indeed much, of our writing. The contexts in which we live out our personal lives and carry on our professional work – temples and churches, hostels and prisons, personal encounters and public occasions – interweave with other forms of encounter and inspiration: works of art, painting, sculpture and music.

Hebrew/Christian scripture has quite explicitly brought both shape and content to Mark's and Nicola's poetry in different ways. As poetry published or shared in congregations and communities, much of this work finds expression in liturgical use in mainstream churches and more experimental, innovative settings. Mark's editorial and translation work as a poet gathering together and arranging poems from both 'secular' sources and Christian tradition provides contemporary churches with poetry resources that interpret and illuminate scripture in public worship and in the practice of personal devotion. Nicola's work as a feminist liturgist has enabled a particular channelling of the poetic voice into contexts in which women and men are seeking new forms of public ritual and prayer.

For the reader it may be hoped that the sound of five differing voices will echo, re-echo and reverberate, creating the surround sound, the edgeless 'bigness' of realities which are beyond grammar. For all of us this volume marks a rite of passage. For Ruth, Mark and Nicola poetry has been a part of their professional repertoire. Ruth has led writing classes in a variety of contexts, including prisons; Mark draws on poetry in leading Quiet Days and retreats, in teaching theology as well as helping clergy and others to reflect on the experience of professional practice; similarly, Nicola's teaching frequently draws on poetry, as does her work in conducting retreats, and she has developed a particular commitment to using women's poetry as a means of empowerment for women in search of the sacred. Alongside this public location for poetry as it speaks into the community of faith or the professional, educational spheres there is also the more intimate place of poetry which has its location as a personal means of expression to be shared in the artistic exchange of small groups of poets, occasional readings and personal communication.

In part the commitment to producing this book resulted from our shared, deepening realisation of the importance to participants in our classes and groups of engaging with spirituality's articulation as poetry while also discovering poetry's rootedness both in faith and in its felt absences. Ruth's time as poet-in-residence in a school for students with learning difficulties helped her to understand that the feel, shape and sound of a poem conveyed meaning, sometimes religious meaning, in ways that words alone cannot. Nicola and Eleanor were stirred and exhilarated by the response and creativity of participants in a course entitled 'Poetry as Pilgrimage' at Woodbrooke Quaker Study Centre, Birmingham, UK in 2012. Gavin has used poetry in catechesis and has run day retreats on poetry and art as prayer, exploring some of the ways in which both art and poetry may help us to pray. He has also written a poetry-laden script for the BBC morning worship which led to the Diviners' working as a group for the BBC. Mark's collaboration as a poet with other theologians (biblical scholar Paula Gooder and practical theologian James Woodward) in writing reflections on the four Gospels (Woodward, Gooder and Pryce, 2011, 2012, 2013, forthcoming 2014) shows the powerful role that poetry can play alongside other theological approaches in interpreting scripture and strengthening the life of prayer and faith.

The task of preparing this book has impelled or at least allowed each of us to track down poetry's part in our lives over some five decades and to discern ways in which poetry offers and discloses a unity between our personal and professional selves. We found ourselves acknowledging the significance of being a part of a community of practice – the Diviners (and in some cases other critically supportive poetry groups too). At the same time this current project suggests possibilities for meeting with many more people for whom poetry and spirituality are significant.

Our hope is that this book will be of interest to both poets and theologians, to all who read poetry and are interested in the connections between literature and faith, but also to those seeking new inspiration for preaching, liturgy and pastoral care, and to those committed to the practice and nurturing of a contemplative attitude to life in which profound attention and respect are offered to words and to the creative Word at work in the world and in all creatures. Informed by the poets' autobiographies, writing practices and diverse Christian backgrounds, as well as by scholarship and experience, the contributions open up many issues for exploration and reflection: the nature of creativity and the distinction between divine and human creation; the creative process as a process of exploration, epiphany and revelation; craft and labour in the writing process; the forging and problematising of identity through the writing process; the diverse ways in which art (in this case, poetry) can reflect, challenge and be in dialogue with faith, and the ways in which faith can inform and challenge art; the exercise of power and voice in both poetry and faith and ways in which race, gender, culture and other such factors interact and shape poetic and theological discourse; and many more themes, some of which, doubtless, we ourselves are only dimly aware of.

In what follows, through a mixture of poetry and prose, we seek to evoke something of the elusive and compulsive process of divining sacred words. We invite our readers to discover the mysterious process of making nothing happen.

References

Astley, Neil and Pamela Robertson-Pearce (eds), *Soul Food: Nourishing Poems for Starved Minds* (Tarset: Bloodaxe, 2007)

Atwan, Robert, George Dardess and Peggy Rosenthal (eds), *Divine Inspiration: The Life of Jesus in World Poetry* (New York/Oxford: Oxford University Press, 1998)

Atwan, Robert and Laurance Wieder (eds), *Chapters into Verse: A Selection of Poetry in English Inspired by the Bible from Genesis through Revelation* (Oxford/New York: Oxford University Press, 2000)

Auden, W. H, 'In Memory of W.B. Yeats', *Collected Poems*, edited by Edward Mendelson (London: Faber & Faber, 2007, revised edition)

Batchelor, Mary (ed.), *The Lion Christian Poetry Collection* (Oxford: Lion, 1995)

Bowker, John, *Hallowed Ground: Religions and the Poetry of Place* (London: SPCK, 1993)

Countryman, William, *The Poetic Imagination: An Anglican Spiritual Tradition* (London: DLT, 1999)

Edwards, David, *Poets and God: Chaucer, Shakespeare, Herbert, Milton, Wordsworth, Coleridge, Blake* (London: DLT, 2005)

Griffiths, Richard, *Poetry and Prayer* (London/New York: Continuum, 2005)

Guite, Malcolm, *Faith, Hope and Poetry: Theology and the Poetic Imagination* (Aldershot: Ashgate, 2012)

Hart, David (ed.) *Is a Religious Poem Possible in the Early 21st Century?* (Alvechurch: Flarestack, 2004)

Housden, Roger, *Ten Poems to Change Your Life* (London: Hodder & Stoughton, 2002)

Housden, Roger, *Ten Poems to Set You Free* (New York: Harmony, 2003)

Housden, Roger, *Ten Poems to Change Your Life – Again and Again* (New York: Harmony, 2007)

Morley, Janet, *The Heart's Time: A Poem a Day for Lent and Easter* (London: SPCK, 2011)

Woodward, James, Paula Gooder and Mark Pryce, *Journeying with Mark* (London: SPCK, 2011)

Woodward, James, Paula Gooder and Mark Pryce, *Journeying with Luke* (London: SPCK, 2012)

Woodward, James, Paula Gooder and Mark Pryce, *Journeying with Matthew* (London: SPCK, 2013)

Woodward, James, Paula Gooder and Mark Pryce, *Journeying with John* (London: SPCK, forthcoming 2014)

Chapter 1

(W)riting like a Woman: In Search of a Feminist Theological Poetics

Nicola Slee

Introduction

In what follows, I want to tell something of how poetry and faith have been significant in my life and how I perceive their interrelationship. Underlying this story is a sense that both poetry and theology have funded and nourished my sense of self from earliest days – taught me who I am, where I belong in the world and how to speak into and of the world. At the same time, poetry and theology have been arenas in which I've struggled to come to authentic speech as a woman – a pervasive theme in much second-wave feminist writing from the 1960s onwards, where there has been considerable debate about what it means to write, think and speak (even throw and climb!) 'as' or 'like a woman'.[1] The debate has centred around women's struggles to find an authentic female tradition or traditions of writing, to take up a subject position (rather than be the object of the male gaze or male writing) and to develop distinctively feminine forms of literature without buying into limited, essentialist notions of gender. My own struggle has been to find traditions of theology and poetry into which my own particular voice can speak and to find a way of integrating poetic and theological discourse, without prioritising one over the other or re-inscribing oppressive dualisms – emotion versus intellect, concretion versus abstraction, feminine versus masculine – onto the poetry/theology relation.

---

[1]   Themes of silence and voice have been pursued in feminist literary criticism, feminist psychology and feminist theology, e.g., Olsen (1978), Rich (1980), Gilligan (1982), Ruether (1983) and Belenky et al. (1986). For discussion of throwing, reading and writing 'as' or 'like' a woman/man, see Kamuf (1980), Young (1980), Culler (1982), Lovell (1983), Scholes (1987) and Chisholm (2008).

In this piece, I seek to write in a way that is confessional and reflexive, as well as thematic, as a way of honouring this struggle and attempting to hold the tension between different modes of thinking and speaking. My aim is to stay close to my experience of both reading and writing poetry, as well as to draw on my commitment to prayer and public liturgy, my work of teaching theology and spirituality (in which poetry has a place), and my research into women's faith lives (which employs ethnography in ways that link with poetry), for it is out of these contexts that my own writing has been shaped and to which it seeks to speak. I shall also make some reference to the wider feminist literature that has pursued the discussion about what 'writing like a woman' can mean.

Poetry and Prayer: Language of the Depths

Poetry and faith have always been there, from as far back as I can remember, and have always been intertwined, though it is perhaps only with hindsight that I can recognise how significant have been their interconnections – and these have not always been capable of articulation, precisely because the roots of each go deep and have been as much lived as reflected upon, wellsprings of vitality and creativity that have not required inspection. Part of the attraction, as well as the challenge, of writing this piece and engaging in the collective enterprise of this book, is to seek to find a way of unearthing and articulating the relationship between poetry and faith which might go at least some way towards doing justice to their depths, without killing off what remains elusive, mysterious and properly beyond rationalisation.

I wasn't brought up in a particularly literary household, but my upbringing was one that gave me an instinctual, uncomplicated love of language, poetry, rhythm and music. Both my parents were compelled to leave school in their early teens, but both sides of my family held as precious the written and spoken word, and handed on to me different forms of literary and religious tradition which shaped my sense of self, community and world. My Scottish mother came from a generation that learnt poetry by heart and recited reams of the Border poets to me and my siblings, as well as classics of the English canon, in her broad brogue. I didn't understand much of it, but I loved the *sound* of it and the way it made the hairs stand up on the back of my neck; I imbibed the sense that words are visceral things, and can *do* things – charm, sooth, rouse, amaze, infuriate, lodge in the body and subconscious in such a way as to continue their mysterious reverberations. From as far back as I can remember, I was taken to the Methodist chapel a mile along the road from where we lived – largely peopled by my Devonian father's relatives – where I heard the King James Version read Sunday by Sunday and sang rousing Wesley hymns. I learnt something about the reverence and holiness of words, the respect sacred texts were accorded, but also the love of scripture and hymnody.

These early formative experiences root the sense I have always had that poetry and prayer are very close to each other, are both forms of speaking that, as Dorothee Soelle puts it, 'place us into relation with the ground of the depth of being' (2003: 32). There is a quality of attentiveness, of language honed to the essential in both poetry and prayer that I recognised in the rather motley mix of Robbie Burns, Moody and Sankey hymnody and the cadences of the King James Bible that made up my child's repertoire of tongues. In each of these different forms of oral poetry, I experienced something of the out-of-the-ordinariness of poetic diction, the denseness and compactness of words working at full tilt, the intricacy of sound patterns and rhythms that didn't need to be spelt out to me because they were doing their own magical stuff. They also taught me something of the discipline and restraint of poetic speech, of language working with the spaces, pauses and silences between and beneath the words.

Both poetry and prayer are more than the words themselves – they call us to something else, *someone* else perhaps, above and beyond the words – and they do this as much by what is *not said* as by what is said, by their rhythms and sounds and patterns as well as their obvious content. The gaps and pauses in poems, as well as in liturgy, are breathing spaces, fertile places where the words take on extra freight. For me, the sound of poetry is extremely important and I often *hear* the first line of a new poem, as if spoken to me from another source (although it is, of course, my own self speaking); the sound of the line leads me into the whole poem, often without any conscious sense of what it is I am writing until after I have written it. There is a sense, which perhaps all poets feel, that one's own work comes from a deeper source than the conscious self and knows more than the conscious self knows. As Adrienne Rich has written, 'poems are like dreams, in them you put what you don't know you know' (1980: 40). The poetic word, like God's creative *dhabar* that utters the world into being in Genesis, is a fiat, a performative word that does what it speaks. Thus a poem works, as much through its subliminal impact on the ear, the memory and the unconscious as on its appeal to the rational mind. I have learnt to appreciate that the 'meaning' of a poem is far more than any moral, religious or political 'message' that might be summarised on the basis of the poem. Any poem that can be translated into prose terms without loss, is hardly a poem worthy of the name. The poem is a totality of sound, rhythm, association, image and voice, of which the surface 'meaning' is only one perhaps relatively insignificant dimension – which is why, perhaps, 'nonsense' poems have such appeal on the one hand and, on the other, it is more or less impossible to say exactly why and how a poem makes an impact on one person but not on another. David Constantine (2004: 326) suggests that: 'A poem, like the clitoris, is there / For pleasure'. The sensuous discourse of poetry by and large eschews abstraction and philosophical distance (although plenty of poems are intellectually demanding) in favour of concretion. 'For all the history of grief / An empty doorway and a maple leaf' (MacLeish, 1985: 106). Constantine's sexual metaphor also suggests that poetry belongs to the realm of the feminine and to the female body – themes to which I will return.

We could speak of this sensual particularity of poetry in theological terms as coming close to what Christians understand by incarnation and sacrament, themselves an outworking of the doctrine of creation[2] which speaks of the physical world as an expression of the being and longing-to-be-in-relation of God. The universe is created, not as some kind of extension of God, but as something that is truly its own self, multiple and various and complex as it is, free to be separate and apart from God, and yet imbued with the qualities and characteristics of its maker. All artists know something of this relation between themselves as creators and the work of art as an independent, separate thing-in-itself which must be let go to live its own life in the world, and yet which has emerged from the being of the creator and is an authentic expression of the person. In incarnation, as in creation, God gives Godself to the created order without reservation, in total vulnerability and trust, in openness and in commitment, in self-giving and in love – and this giving is expressed in God being born in human flesh, becoming a discrete, particular, embodied part of the creation, subject to all its limitations and laws. The God who

---

[2]   See Gavin's chapter in this collection for an elaboration on the theology of creation.

is the source and origin of all that is becomes a newborn whelp, utterly dependent on other creatures for very existence. This bespeaks a divine self-offering that gives to the uttermost, that risks not only rejection but annihilation. If there is some kind of aesthetic parallel to incarnation in the work and life of the poet, it is perhaps to be seen in the costly struggle the poet must wage with the slippery and intractable stuff that is language in order to compress the most profound experiences and apprehensions of the self into a frail, limited body that is the poem. Every poem, we might say, gestures towards incarnation and has a sacramental quality about it, insofar as it succeeds in becoming a vehicle for revelation, a place where grace and truth are compressed and encountered.[3]

This is the kind of second-order theological reflection on poetic creation that has only come later, after decades of writing and reading poetry, as I have learnt to stand back from the process in order to reflect on it. Nevertheless, it is clear to me that my own poetry is deeply embedded within, and nurtured by, the specific forms and texts of the Christian scriptures and liturgy, particularly Anglican forms of worship but also other, more experimental and 'alternative' forms of liturgical expression. Much of my poetry addresses consciously 'religious' subjects, stories and texts, has often been written for liturgical use, and even when neither of these is true, draws deeply on scriptural forms – particularly the language and rhythms of the psalms (repetition, parallelism, chorus and so on) and makes use of liturgical forms such as the confession, canticle and litany. I include in the poems that follow examples that draw explicitly on liturgical forms and settings ('A litany for illiterate girls', 'At the table of Christa', 'How to pray') and others that, while not making the connection explicit, have the sounds and the intentionality of prayer and liturgy behind or within them ('Sea song', 'Anna', 'The river').

Much of my poetry, perhaps all of it, is written, whether consciously or not, against the backdrop of divine presence or absence and is addressed, whether consciously or not, to a divine 'Thou'. My poems, as well as more overtly liturgical texts, are constantly in search of more authentic ways of addressing, naming or evoking the Thou who becomes, not less mysterious and elusive with time, but more. I find myself returning to certain elemental images – water, the sea, the abyss, darkness, the erotic, the wilderness, death – in poems that gesture

---

[3] This is perhaps less true in certain kinds of epic, narrative poetry than in lyric poetry, though even in long poems this element of compression is present.

towards the divine (and this is obvious in the poems that follow), but also drawing on more playful terms and names for God: God as stroppy middle-aged mother, as hiker, spinster, quester, jester, as the female Christ figure, the Christa who, herself, appears in many diverse forms. I am also learning to be more adventurous in the voices, tones and forms I use in my poetry, moving out from a predominant use of the contemplative, respectful stance of the worshipper from which much of my earlier poetry was written, to occupy a greater range of stances – the sceptical, the quizzical, the angry, the humorous, the stoical. In the poems that follow, I've included a range of tones and voices: the erotic, passionate voice of 'Writing the body' and 'Banquet', the ironic humour of 'It's a girl', the reflective, contemplative stance of 'How to pray' and 'The river', the lyrical attitude towards the ordinary in 'Morning tea', the angry protest of 'The mother's rage', the exploration of loss in 'Rummage' and 'Envoys', as well as the praise and adoration of 'Sea song'. Nor, of course, should the poet's voice be assumed to represent the 'I' of the person who writes, at least not in any direct, confessional sense. Although much of my own writing is, in fact, strongly confessional, I have also experimented with the dramatic monologue as a form for inhabiting other voices, particularly as a way of bringing to voice the anonymous, invisible or ignored women of scripture, tradition and the contemporary world (a strategy common amongst feminist poets and liturgists, see below). 'Anna' and 'The mother's rage' are examples of this approach.

Interestingly, much contemporary British poetry is written in a tone of detached, ironic distance – more than is the case in contemporary American verse, say – and the use of the passionate voice in poetry, including a religious voice of adoration and worship, is rare. Yet if, as Penelope Shuttle suggests, part of the purpose of the poet is 'to go on loving the world', even 'when it deals you severe blows' (Shuttle, 2006), then the voice of praise and blessing needs to be present in contemporary poetry, however mediated and translated. This is a language that is basic to religion, and part of what religious poets have to offer the wider contemporary scene might be a capacity to bless the world and all that is in it. Yet for a language of blessing to be authentic in the contemporary world, it needs to speak to those for whom religious vocabulary and speech are not only foreign but also empty and redundant, devoid of symbolic force. It is notable that many contemporary poets, most of them without overt religious faith, frequently employ religious or liturgical forms to address weighty matters, investing them with new, secular meaning at the same time as calling on and utilising their ancient, totemic power for their own meanings and ends. Carol Ann Duffy's much-anthologised sonnet, 'Prayer' (1994), composed of entirely secular expressions of what might be considered forms of prayer, is an obvious example of this tendency of secular poets to pick up and use traditional, religious forms. Adam Zagajewski's 'Try to praise the mutilated world' (2001), published in *The New Yorker* in the aftermath of the Twin Towers' collapse on 9/11, is another.

Just as in the wider cultural setting there are myriad ways of religious faith and poetry speaking to, or drawing from, each other, so in my own development as a poet and a theologian, the ways I have experienced and understood the relationship between poetry and faith have shifted and changed. The intertwining of poetry and religion continued throughout childhood and into adolescence, where it became more tutored and self-conscious. My schooling introduced me to a sampling of the riches of the Western canon of literature, with all its glories and limitations. English was always my first love in school, although I was intensely pious too and I'd have been hard pressed to choose between the Bible and the great religious poets (John Donne, George Herbert and most especially Gerard Manley Hopkins were my heroes). I was also learning more about a critical study of religious texts through Theology 'A' level, though it took me years to permit critical theological reflection to shape and inform my practice of faith. When I came to have to decide what to read at university, I finally opted for Theology because I knew that I'd never stop reading literature and poetry, whereas if I had chosen Literature, I doubt I would have carried on reading much theology. Indeed, when at university, I often used to bunk off theology lectures to sneak into the English department to hear poets and literary critics. So there was always this pull between religion and literature, sometimes experienced as a tension or something I needed to choose between (as if it was not possible to have them both!) – but they were always both there, speaking to each other, informing each other, feeding each other or fighting with each other.

Throughout childhood and adolescence, too, I was writing poetry. Most of it was undoubtedly terrible; although we did do written composition at school, no-one seemed to think there was any need to instruct us in the craft of writing. It was either something one could do, or not. Both writing and faith now seem to me essentially disciplines to be practised rather than a therapeutic outpouring of thoughts and feelings (on the page, to God), and much of this can be learnt – or at least improved – by practice. Both prayer and poetry are a repeated practice concerned with as profound an attentiveness as I can muster (as Simone Weil has characterised the essence of prayer in her classic (1977) study): attentiveness to my own life, both inner and outer, as well as attentiveness to other people, objects and events in all their mysterious otherness, and in and through each of these, attentiveness to the source of all life and creativity, the Word uncreated and incarnate.

Feminist Critique and Struggle: Learning to Write and Pray 'Like a Woman'

At some stage in my developing love affair with poetry and theology, there began a gradual conscientisation process as I became increasingly aware of the deeply patriarchal nature, both of the religious tradition I was part of and the literary/ cultural heritage I was steeped in. I began to realise in my early twenties how the texts and traditions I'd inherited and that had formed me were largely those of a privileged Western male elite. While many of my teachers had been women, all the poets I'd learnt about and read were male, with the exception of Christina Rossetti and Sylvia Plath. With one or two notable exceptions, all my theology teachers were men, and certainly all the texts and ideas I was introduced to were from male writers and thinkers. I could not have named a single female theologian – it had not dawned on me even to ask the question of whether any existed. The only exception to this gaping female absence was being introduced to the writings of Julian of Norwich while I was working in my gap year at Lee Abbey in North Devon and, through her, to the existence of other medieval women mystics. But neither Julian nor any of the other female saints featured in my theology degree. At that time, in the late seventies, feminist theology was only just beginning to emerge, not in academia at first but in small, grassroots networks of which I began to be a part. Groups like Women in Theology (a national network for women wanting to explore theology in new ways), as well as local and regional groups, met to do theology in a wide variety of ways, employing methods borrowed from academia (seminars, lectures and so on) but also using the arts, imaginative forms of reflection, body work, therapeutic methods, role-play and so on as a way of seeking to engage politically and holistically with emerging feminist theologies.[4] In company with other women who were part of this early feminist theological and liturgical movement, I found myself writing in a variety of modes as an expression of feminist theological exploration. My first published article (Slee, 1984) was a re-reading of the parables of Jesus from the perspective of women's experience, and this seems significant because the parables themselves might be seen as a prime scriptural form which combines the poetic and the conceptual, provocative metaphors (whether brief, riddle-like koans or more developed, narrative forms) that engage imagination, brain, heart and will. At the same time, I was writing poems and prayer-texts, often for collective use in feminist theology and worship groups. Much of the content of my first collection (Slee, 2004a), though published much later, comes from this period.

Throughout my twenties and thirties, then, I kept both poetry and faith alive – or should I say they kept me alive? I was deeply engaged in both, but sometimes inhabited them as if they were separate compartments, coming from different parts of me: the rational versus the affective, the professional versus the personal, the academic versus the spiritual. Theology was associated with the former, poetry with the latter (though personal faith was more akin to poetry, being associated with feelings, an intense personal relationship with God, and so on). There was, for a long time, a huge split between these different parts of myself, and the tension created by this produced enormous paralysis – a big theme of my twenties and thirties. I was working – or trying to work – in two modes, two forms of writing: the academic and scholarly, on the one hand, and poetic and liturgical on the other; both were essential and yet I experienced them as pulling in different directions, and it was almost impossible to keep both alive at the same time. When I engaged in scholarly writing, the poems seemed to die a death and go far away, underground, and much of my own imaginative life and creative power died with them. When the poems returned – often with ferocious, almost violent, assertiveness, bringing havoc and a painful return of feeling in their wake – they were greedy in their demands and would only accept centre-stage, not content to share the limelight with my academic writing.

---

[4] For an account of the development of feminist theology networks in the UK, see Daggers (2002).

This experience of struggle between different parts of the self and different forms of writing is not, I have come to recognise, merely a private or personal dilemma – one of the reasons for recounting it here in some detail. The struggle to overcome false polarities and to forge an authentic 'voice' that does not simply re-inscribe the dualisms is a recurring theme in the lives of many other women students, scholars and writers – something I explored in my doctoral research into women's faith lives, where metaphors and narratives of alienation, paralysis and dividedness were pervasive (Slee, 2004b). It has been a major theme in both literary and theological feminist discourse, addressed in rather different ways by Anglo-American feminists and French feminists such as Hélène Cixous, Julia Kristeva and Luce Irigaray. Embedded within an intellectual tradition of French philosophy and psychoanalytic theory, French feminists have sought to respond to Jacques Lacan's thesis that postulates the symbolic order of language as essentially masculine, dominated by the phallic Law of the Father. In Lacan's scheme, language, rationality itself and all that flows from them – law, religion, science and civilisation – are structured by the masculine symbolic. The feminine has no subjectivity or voice within this order, but is relegated to the realm of the unconscious. In Lacanian terms, to speak at all is to enter the masculine realm and women themselves have no language of their own. As Grace Jantzen (1998: 42) puts it, 'in order to speak, women must use men's language, play by men's rules, find themselves in a foreign country with an alien tongue'. Exploring this theme in a highly concrete fashion, Elaine Showalter argued that, in the American university system of the early 1970s, women students were taught to 'think like a man'; studying texts and traditions supposedly representative of the best of the literary canon, women students were 'estranged from their own experience and unable to perceive its shape and authenticity'. Expected 'to identify as readers with a masculine experience and perspective … presented as the human one', women students learnt to doubt and even hate their own selves, becoming 'timid, cautious and insecure' when enjoined to 'think for themselves' (Showalter, 1971: 855–7).

What, then, does it mean to write or think 'as a woman', and how may women claim a space – a room, a tradition and a voice – of their own? This is the central question of 1980s feminism, and even though in more recent debate gender has been radically destabilised by theorists such as Judith Butler (1990), as well as by increasing awareness of the complexity and fluidity of gender identities and relations, the question is still a fruitful and creative one for the female writer – at least for this one.

Feminists themselves propose various solutions to the dilemma of 'writing as/ like a woman'. Cixous, Irigaray and Kristeva all, to some extent, accept Lacan's thesis of language and culture as the realm of the masculine yet, at the same time, seek to disrupt and subvert it through a range of creative, writerly and linguistic strategies. Cixous proclaims woman as the source of life, power and energy and announces the advent of a new, female form of language – écriture féminine – which subverts the patriarchal binary. In 'The Laugh of the Medusa', she urges women to 'put herself into the text', to 'write her self', to 'write as a woman, toward women', claiming the female body as the source of their writing (Cixous, 1976: 875). Irigaray offers a variety of tactics that she believes can undercut phallocentric logic: mimeticism, or the mimicry of male discourse; female mysticism understood as a space in Western history where women have spoken and acted publicly, and 'le parler femme' or 'womanspeak', a spontaneous form of feminine speech that emerges when women speak together. Kristeva proposes a new distinction between the 'semiotic' and the 'symbolic', to replace Lacan's distinction between the Imaginary and the Symbolic Order, and reconceives their relation. The symbolic represents the network of signifiers which constitutes language and culture (identified with the masculine), while the semiotic represents the physical basis of language – 'its sounds, cadences, tones, and rhythms, originating in the body' (Jantzen, 1998: 195) and identified with the maternal feminine. For Kristeva, the monolithic structure of the symbolic 'can be disrupted by the irrepressible semiotic with its multiple meanings and sounds … The sober intellectual narrative where words and meanings are rigorously pinned down is subverted by the rhythms, intonations, repetitions, and sound-plays of the semiotic, which is a *jouissance*, a "transgression" of the symbolic order' (Jantzen, 1998: 196).

The struggle for the woman writer, the woman thinker, is how to inhabit patriarchal discourse without doing fundamental violence to her sense of self, without reinforcing her very absence and silence or positioning herself as stereotypically 'feminine' – passive, receptive, occupying the affective domain, maternal and caring (roles which, of course, religion has legitimised and theologised over centuries). In order to speak or think at all, the woman writer has to find a new language, make new maps, revise and reverse the patriarchal myths – and Kristeva in particular considers poetry, with its roots in ritual, to have a peculiar potency to subvert and recreate the symbolic order. Adrienne Rich, one of the foremost feminist poets and thinkers whose work can be seen as a forging of just such a new form of discourse, speaks of the profound alienation experienced by the woman poet: 'The rules break like a thermometer ... the maps they gave us were out of date / by years' (Rich, 1993: 31). The female poet, like the political agent, is required to exercise 'radical imagination' – 'the radical imagination of the not-yet, the what-if' (Prince, 1998:1) – in order to give birth to new forms of perception, new ways of speaking. Even while, in more recent debate, critics have problematised the notion of 'writing like a woman' (or, indeed, a man), just as gender itself has been radically destabilised by theorists such as Judith Butler (1990), the exploration of how gender is constructed in texts is still a fruitful and creative one.

Feminist poets, like feminist theologians, have found themselves engaged in many kinds of critical and revisionary tactics in order to remake the language. Both poets and theologians have employed invective, lament, irony and humour to undo the assumptions of patriarchal texts and traditions, and feminist liturgies of denunciation and protest use such strategies. Both poets and theologians have revisited patriarchal (including scriptural) texts and stories, rewriting them from different perspectives of female protagonists: Carol Ann Duffy's (1999) *The World's Wife* is a recent example in poetry, Sara Maitland (1987, 1995) has employed the medium of the short story to do the same thing in fiction, and feminist biblical hermeneutics, from Elizabeth Cady Stanton's ground-breaking *Women's Bible* onwards (1895, 1898), provide myriad examples of this tactic in theological mode. Rich, in a much-quoted essay, described this kind of 're-vision' by women as 'an act of survival' (1980: 35). My own attempts to re-write biblical or liturgical texts from a female perspective – of which my poems 'Anna', 'The mother's rage', 'It's a girl', 'Christa in the wilderness' and 'At the table of Christa' are examples – stand firmly within this tradition of feminist revisionist mythology. Yet, although there are many parallels between the work and intentions of feminist poets, fiction writers and theologians, there is little literature addressing the relationship between feminism, literature and theology[5] – another reason, perhaps, why many of us have struggled to integrate these forms within our own work and lives.

---

[5]   There are, of course, some significant exceptions; for example, Susan Alicia Ostriker (1987) and, in the UK, the work of Heather Walton (2007a, 2007b).

Poetry as a Means of Prayer and Theological Reflection: A Place of Integration

Integration of the forms and voices, then, has become an urgent and dominant concern of my middle years. Gradually, over the past decade or so, more or less successfully, I've begun to integrate theology, poetry, spirituality and feminism into my own life as some kind of a whole. My writing, I hope, mirrors something of this integration but is also the place where I practise it. The work of integration has been, at one level, a slow, developmental process of trial and error, but it has also required some particular choices, including some refusals of inauthentic ways of being/writing/speaking as well as some options for greater risk-taking, visibility and putting-myself-out-there – not only in my writing, but also in my teaching, public speaking and life choices. I had to lay down a long, painfully abortive attempt to write the definitive PhD thesis, give up trying to please daddy (gain approval in the male academy) in order to release a more authentic writing voice which expressed itself both in poetry and in a more engaged feminist practical theology. Having aborted one endlessly protracted, dryly theoretical PhD, I began another, this time employing qualitative research methods as a way of listening to women speak about their spiritual lives and analysing their metaphors, narratives and ways of speaking as a way of discerning pattern and shape within them. This piece of research became a forum for the work of integration as I drew on scholarly literature from theology, psychology, literary studies and feminism and developed a method of data analysis that read interview transcripts in similar ways to the ways I read poems, paying close attention to vocabulary, rhythm, metre and imagery, as well as to the gaps and silences within the text. Although at this stage I was not aware of it, there is a growing interest in such a use of poetry in data analysis in the qualitative paradigm (see, for example, Furnam, Lietz and Langer, 2006). Poetry was coming out of the intensely personal realm of my 'private life' and 'going public' as I employed *poesis* as part of my research methodology.

Not long after completing the doctorate, I published my first collection of poems, prayers and liturgical texts under the title, *Praying Like a Woman*. At the time, this felt like an enormous exposure of the self, with nowhere to hide and the risk of disapproval from the male hierarchy (both ecclesial and academic). Yet this risking of the poetic voice freed me to rediscover a more authentic theological mode of writing. Theology gradually moved out of the realm of (someone else's) abstract, clever ideas into the language of poetry, prayer and liturgy. With many feminists, I am convinced that 'the master's tools will never dismantle the master's house', as Audre Lorde (1996: 158) famously put it. If theology and poetry are to be capable of bearing women's lives and meanings, their forms will have to change. It is not enough to simply 'add women and stir' to existing patriarchal traditions, whether we are talking about literature or theology. The traditions themselves have to be dismantled, recreated and re-formed, with women finding new ways of speaking, thinking and writing – from the body, from our own diverse realities, from our own sense of the sacred. These are themes that are at the heart of feminist theology and literature, of course, and with which much of my own writing has been intensely engaged. My poem, 'Writing the body', seeks to explore and interrelate these themes. Drawing on Cixous's 'Laugh of the Medusa' (1975), I seek to suggest how writing as a woman, from a woman's body, is connected both with 'righting' the body – the long, painful process of undoing and correcting patriarchal control of female bodiliness, sexuality and self-expression – and 'riting' the body: ritualising women's experiences through lament, celebration, feminist sacrament and ritual actions. The title of this chapter is also intended to gesture towards these interconnections.

Bringing poetry more and more into my teaching, public speaking and retreat work has also been an important part of the journey towards integration, and I have become self-conscious in my intention to utilise the tradition(s) of women's spiritual poetry in my teaching. These traditions are much less known, in both theological and poetry circles, than the canon of men's religious poetry. A number of commentators have traced the English tradition of men's religious poetry, in which the Anglican poet priest has a particular part (Countryman, 1999; Guite, 2012), and I would want to place alongside this a much more diffuse and hidden tradition of women's religious/Christian poetry, which has been, of necessity, until very recently, a lay and therefore less 'official' tradition. The work of women poets such as Stevie Smith (1975), Kathleen Raine (2000), Elizabeth Jennings (2002), Denise Levertov (2003), and many others,[6] has been enormously important in my own development as a woman poet who chooses to write about faith and spirituality, legitimising and demonstrating some of the range of ways in which

---

[6] For examples of collections of women's spiritual/religious poetry, see Sewell (1991, 1996), Zundel (1991), Neuberger (1992) and Hirshfield (1994).

women can write about faith *as women*, in and through the particular lenses of their own embodied lives. I have also found that bringing women's poetry into the classroom, the pulpit and the retreat centre, is a potentially liberating and empowering force in women's lives. Hearing, engaging with and responding to women's poetry can be a key means for women students and seekers to have the courage to claim their own voices and speak their own truth. Over many years, I have been running retreats and courses for women (as well as some for mixed gender groups) that explore spirituality in contemporary women's poetry. Again and again, I have discovered how the words, as well as the lives, of women poets, can speak profoundly to contemporary spiritual seekers, offering not only a language to express the inarticulate struggles and hopes of women in search of the sacred, but also a company of sisters who have walked the way of faith before and have forged authentic expression for their own faith lives. It is not, of course, that men's poetry cannot also speak to, and nourish, women; I would not be without the poetry of Donne, Herbert, Hopkins, not to mention R.S. Thomas, Wendell Berry, Charles Causley, and many others. Yet, for a woman of faith seeking my own language of faith, men's language alone cannot substitute for the women's tradition I need to know and inhabit. Nor is gender, of course, the only relevant factor. I am conscious that most of the poets I have mentioned as significant in my own development are white and British, reflecting the bias of my own education and reading. Nevertheless, black poets such as Maya Angelou (1995), Alice Walker (2005) and Jean 'Binta' Breeze (2011) are also part of the great tradition of women poets I have more recently discovered and would wish to celebrate and affirm.

So, without really planning to do so, I realise that I've come, over more recent years, to use poetry quite deliberately and intentionally as a means of doing theology from my own specific context and location as a feminist Christian in search of women's literary as well as religious traditions and seeking to forge a contemporary feminist theological poetics. Poetry offers a form of theological reflection and exploration that allows me to work with a multiplicity of sources, experiences and questions, in a disciplined yet playful, even subversive kind of way, with a freedom and quality of intense engagement that is less easy (for me, at least) to sustain in prose. Poetry has become a medium in which to explore some key theological questions, and to do so drawing on some of the same sources that theologians use (scripture, tradition – in the form of doctrines, creedal statements, visual images, lives of the saints and so on – and academic theology itself) but engaging them in a more free-flowing, unsystematic, episodic kind of way.

Sometimes a passage of scripture might be the starting point for a poem (as was the case for 'Banquet' and 'Anna' below); sometimes an idea, suggestive phrase or image from a theological text might prompt the poem (as is the case for many of the poems in my *Book of Mary* and *Seeking the Risen Christa*). Along with many contemporary poets, a visual image or artefact can often invite poetic response: I wrote a sequence of poems in response to Jake Lever's stunning series of hands paintings, one of which is included in the selection below.[7] 'Chapter house women' was also one of a sequence of poems responding to various aspects of Southwell Minster; essentially a 'list poem', the poem lists some of the many different forms and faces of women sculpted into the famous Chapter House at Southwell (see http://www.southwellminster.org/leaves-of-southwell.html). Poetry has been the place where I've wrestled with what it means to 'pray like a woman', not by reflecting on this question in any kind of systematic, second-order way (though I have also done that), but precisely by writing prayers that are grounded in the reality of my own life and that attempt to speak truthfully about my life (its childlessness, for example, or my struggle with low-level sickness and fatigue). Poetry has helped me to shape a language of prayer that is offered from a stance that is honest – 'with eyes open', to use Marjorie Procter-Smith's (1995) phrase, adopting a posture of standing as often as kneeling, using names and terms towards the divine that seek to honour how I understand and perceive that relation. Thus, along with other feminist liturgists, I find myself using hierarchical terms such as 'Lord' and 'Father' sparingly and critically, if at all, preferring terms that invite mutuality and co-creatorship – Friend, Sister, Christa, and so on – though even new names can also become habitual, unthinking, and constantly need to be subverted and renewed, or held in tension with other images and names for the divine.

After my first collection – a gathering together of pieces written over a 20-year period, crystallising around the theme of *Praying Like a Woman* – I've become more ambitious in my engagement with poetry as a means of theological exploration. I've deliberately set out to write a book of poems, a long sequence, exploring a particular

---

[7]   See www.leverarts.com for examples of Jake's work, though not the specific hands painting which inspired the poem. This can be found on the CD which accompanies Thorpe and Lever (2010).

theological topic or theme – Mary, in the first case (*The Book of Mary*, 2007) and the idea, or image of the female Christ, or Christa, in the second (*Seeking the Risen Christa*, 2011). In either case, I could have set out to explore Mary or the Christa in prose terms – and indeed, both books do contain significant prose passages – but using the poetic medium has encouraged in me a freedom, an imaginative creativity, the possibility of engaging with a wide range of diverse perspectives and voices that would not have been possible in an extended prose treatment. A collection of poems allows there to be space as well as connection between the individual poems – in the same kind of way as, within a single poem, there is connection and space between the stanzas, the lines, the images. This is true, of course, of good prose, though in a different way. Poetry, I think, does it more elusively, more enigmatically, without spelling out so clearly the conceptual or metaphoric patterns. Poems leave the reader to do more of the work than most prose, although there can be a kind of elitism in poetry that I don't admire, a refusal to leave any traces for the reader to follow so that reading a poem becomes a detective work of hunting down all the allusions and references. I have, in my own poetry collections, provided ample notes to indicate at least some of the sources of my poems and to provide links to significant resources which readers might not otherwise access.

Not all poems are written as part of a larger project, and not all my poems are consciously 'about' gender in any obvious way. Poems often arise in response to everyday events as well as to liminal, critical incidents. In recent years, I've found myself writing more poems about my family – the death of a brother, relations with my parents, memories of my childhood in North Devon – and I have included some of these in the selection below. 'Rummage' is a poem about distance, as well as connection, between father and daughter, charting the unspoken love that longs to connect but frequently cannot. 'Morning tea' evokes rituals that pervaded my childhood as well as continuing into the present, and is a kind of homage to the women of my childhood who oiled the wheels of domestic and church life with endless cups of tea and home baking. 'Envoys' and 'The river' are poems that narrate and reflect on the processes of bereavement and grief. These poems are a working with my own particular family history, a way of integrating both the wounds and the gifts of my genetic and familial inheritance. They are not separate from the larger engagement with and critique of patriarchy, so much as a mapping of the intimate setting in which I learnt those larger patterns.

Whether small-scale or large, intimate or public, poetry is for me a form of discourse that holds together and may even on occasion resolve the tensions and opposites of my life. Poetry is a way of speaking and thinking that is rooted in the (female) body, utilising the kind of emotional intelligence that emerges from feeling. Utterly visceral, good poetry also engages the brain and requires the reader to think hard, to bring all the faculties of sense, knowledge and critical acuity to bear on the page. Poetry is a form of discourse in which *desire* plays a key role, in which feeling and passion are often strongly present, though may also be refracted through distillation and reflection – there is no one emotional tone or stance of a poem, any more than there is one topic or form. Poetry, at its best, is a way of speaking and thinking that stays close to narrative and concretion, as of course much scripture and liturgy does, and yet offers the reader symbolic, universal and representative truth through the particularity of the concrete/narrative (we're back to poetry as sacrament). Poetry is a way of speaking and thinking that offers both tight discipline yet huge opportunities for freedom, experimentation and play – it is at one and the same time a very small arena and a vast, free space, a kind of playground of the imagination. Poetry offers a way of speaking and thinking that is authentic yet need not be straightforwardly confessional; it can allow the poet to take on a variety of voices and perspectives, being both 'oneself' and yet moving behind or within other voices and identities, inhabiting multiple perspectives as a way of reflecting truth from different vantage points. Poetry is a way of speaking and thinking that is a close companion to prayer; like prayer, it pushes at the edges of language, it inhabits absence and silence as willingly as the word.

For all these, as well as other, reasons, poetry is a way of speaking and thinking that may be peculiarly fraught with potential for women who seek a form of discourse that integrates the symbolic and the semiotic without having to give up on either. In poetry, language both means/speaks and also stutters, *un*speaks, makes a kind of speaking that is as much non-sense as sense; this is particularly obvious in the work of poets who subvert the usual conventions of meaning-making, who push at the edges of the way words normally work, who play with the sound and arrangement of words and lines on the page. Gertrude Stein's (1990) highly inventive use of repetition, stream of consciousness and bizarre word associations come to mind as an example of poetry functioning at the interface of the symbolic and the semiotic, whose poetic speech likes to inhabit the irrational or the non-rational, speaking with voices that do not make logical sense but proffer other kinds of meanings. Such poetry shares more than a little in common with glossolalia as well as faith's extravagant languages of praise, blessing, lament and confession, all of which may be considered redundant, extraneous, 'making nothing happen' in the world. Yet, for all that, I am encouraged by Grace Jantzen's suggestion, building on Kristeva's analysis, 'that it is from new liturgies and creative metaphor and poetry, in the expansion of a feminist imaginary, not with a preoccupation with truth-claims and justification of beliefs, that the masculinism of Western Christendom can be transformed' (1998: 196).

Perhaps, after all, it is not necessary to have to make a stark choice between the intellectual endeavours of theologians who address themselves to the truth-claims and logical coherence of religious beliefs, on the one hand, and the offerings of poets and liturgists, on the other, who seek to remake the Word that can serve the deepest needs of people's prayer, reflection and action. Both need each other, feed off each other, scrutinise, correct and critique each other, although, if Kristeva is correct in her analysis, it is poetic discourse arising from the semiotic which births the rational thought of the symbolic, rather than the other way round. So perhaps it is necessary to conclude that poetry makes a great deal happen, and births the symbolic systems by which faith lives.

Rummage

'What's this here rummage?' says my dad,
staring at his plateful. Partly it's performance,
the line he knows I'll expect him to say,
presented with a dish of pasta.

'Lasagne', I hear myself answer too primly.
'Go on, you'll enjoy it'.
Like the pizza he and my stepmother still remember
the only time they came to visit me in London.

It's what he can get his tongue around.
Like bowls and cows and how to grow beans
and how many deaths there are
in *The Western Morning News* of people he knows.

It's food, but it could be so much more: the work I do,
the words I've learnt to fill my mouth with, company I keep –
all as exotic as the tangle of peppers, lentils and savoury juices
he doesn't recognise on his plate.

I know he'll not decipher them now.
This is as close as we'll get:
a plateful of pasta and the weight in the air
of all the strangeness he'll never have words for
and I'll never be able to translate.

Sea song[8]

You were colour to me:
bladderwrack and wheatsheaf,
blown meadow and metal rust,
mudflat, oyster.

You were time to me:
morning and evening,
seasons swelling, waning, passing,
all time and no time.

You were sound to me:
whimpering, breathing, singing, hollering,
raging. You held the pippet's thin cry,
stone and mountain's fury.
You were the silence under the mountain.

You were words to me when there were no words,
you were ballast and balm
when everything was unravelling.
You were god to me in a godless time.
You were gentleness.
You were freezing.

How should I speak of you?
As if to tell of my own blood pounding, pulse working.
Time past and time passing,
changed, changing, changeless,
ageing and ageless.

All words drown in you,
as flesh and forest do.
Only the fish live in you
and do not know it.

---

[8]   Previously published in Slee (2004a: 138).

Writing the body[9]

Write the body:
every curve, every nerve, every cell
deserves to be heard,
to be spelled into word, into being.
Mouth her flesh into firm, choice words,
full and round-bellied.
Let the body speak.

Right the body:
untwist, uncurl, unfold
from the tortured conundrums
forced and foisted
for years on her frame.
Throw off the frozen form
she's been locked into
these too long, too cold years.
Unfold. Unbend.
Let her breathe.
Let her mend her ancient ways.
Let her befriend herself again.
Let her live her own
deep, dark and dangerous truth.
She cannot lie.

Rite the body:
sing, dance, fling the body into sacred space.
Charm her, chant her,
cast her into woman-time and pace.
Spell her name.
In this grace she will be born again, over and over.
No stopping her now.
She is bounding out of sight, out of bounds,
like some roaring lioness prowling
the sheer immensity of all space, all time,
leaping the galaxies between the stars.
For there is no stopping her now:
she is coming to herself,
coming into herself,
she is coming
over and over again.

---

[9]   Previously published in Slee (2004a: 97).

Banquet[10]

Song of Songs 2: 4

Like water in the desert you quenched my thirst
Like wine in winter you warmed my belly
Like milk from the breast you satisfied my hunger
Like manna in the wilderness you filled my longing

You were sweet new bread from the oven to my mouth
You were ripe sun-drenched peach to my lips
You were golden lather of honey thick on my tongue
You were clean running water cool on my fingers

All my heart's longing is made known to you
My body's quickening thirst cannot be hidden from you
You sensed the fainting of my flesh and caught me fast in your arms
You lifted my drooping frame and set me at your table of delights

You feasted me right royally at your banquet overflowing with riches
You feted me fondly at your table with your dazzling presence
Until I was full to overflowing
Sated with the sweetness of your love

I am consumed with the taste of your kisses
Drunk with the perfume of your skin
You have fed me with the riches of heaven
You have filled me with the banquet of God

---

[10]   Previously published in Slee (2004a: 113).

How to pray

an empty room
asks to be sat in
for a long time
at different hours of day and night
in many weathers
alone　　　　　　without words

perhaps hold an object in your hands
　　　　a stone
　　　　a cup
　　　　a length of beads
for a long time

or place something well chosen
on the floor or a window ledge
where you will look at it
for a long time

a cup　　a vase　　a stone
a piece of wood

without asking or telling anything
imposing your own shape on the emptiness
as lightly as possible

leave and enter
many times
without disturbing its silences

gradually over many years
a room thus entered and departed
will teach you how to furnish and dispose of
the paraphernalia of a life

Watchers and holy ones

in response to Jake Lever's hands paintings

And God said, Put your golden
child's hand here,
very lightly, over my wise one. I will carry you.

And the child said, Put your old,
leathery hand under mine,
and I will warm it.

And the trees said, Put your aged
human hands and your young children's hands
over our bark to care for us.
We will teach you.

And the darkness said,
Let all the hands rest in us
and cease their doing.
Even the hands of God shall be still.

And it was so.
The hands laid down their hurting
and their praying
and their touching
and their labour
for a time and a season and an age.

And the hands ceased from all their knowing
though nothing was lost.

And the wisdom of the children
and the lovers and the workers
rested in the hands.

And their tongues tolled like bells
though all their fingers were silent.

Anna[11]

I've learnt to live on little.
My body has long forgotten a husband's ardent embraces,
and there were no children to take me into their homes.
My home has become the Temple,
my bed a dark corner under one of the portico's pillars.
I've no possessions to speak of.

I've learnt to live in silence,
every day offering my emptiness up
to mingle with the incense of the sacrifices burning on the altar.
I live on what the pilgrims give me
from the remains of their cooked meat,
when the priests have taken their fill.

I've learnt the passage of time,
how the speeding years
slow to one endless moment
that is never accomplished,
how the mind and the body hold themselves
patiently in readiness
while the waiting goes on growing.

I've learnt how the Word comes,
rising like fire out of the endlessly endured moment
or dropping like a stone
into the stilled mind's surface.

Old as I am, and hollowed out by
prayer and silence and weeping and fasting,
I live for that quickening,
for the pouring that will rise up and overflow all containment,
that my own thirst may be kindled,
my body leap into flame.

In that moment, I'm a young girl again,
and the Word fills my arms like a lover,
sucks at my shrivelled breast like a baby,
pours down my body like fire,
like the dousing of water.

---

[11]   Previously published in Slee (2007: 72–3).

The mother's rage[12]

When *wasn't* I angry, for heaven's sake?
When he arrived at the wrong time in the wrong place
with no midwife close by
nor even clean sheets and water?

Or when we had to make a run for it into Egypt,
my breasts still leaking milk,
my cut vagina still tender?

Or was it earlier, when Joseph threatened to expose me,
abandon me to the villagers' makeshift justice?
God, I hollered the sky down that night.

Or wasn't my rage like a lit bush
when the child disappeared from our straggling caravan
and we had to retrace our steps
up and down the dark alleyways of the city bulging with pilgrims?
I swore he'd feel the back of my hand when we found him.

I was no stranger to fury, let me tell you.
What didn't we have to put up with?
The visions, the voices,
the countless disappearances,
the crazy idiots and hangers-on he brought home with him,
expecting me to feed them and find beds for them all.
The stern visits from the authorities on his trail,
scribes and rabbis spilling their venom at us when they couldn't find him.
The madness of his teaching that threatened to overturn centuries' tradition,
his wild courting of danger.
His harsh refusals to meet us when we went scurrying after him
trying to save him from disaster.
When wasn't I angry?
When didn't my fingers itch to put him across my lap
and teach him a lesson, hard?

I'd give my life for that anger now,
when all that is left to me is weeping and grief
as I cradle his dead body on my lap.

---

[12] Previously published in Slee (2007: 108–9).

Chapter house women[13]

Southwell Minster

Long-nosed, wimpled woman, smirking.
A young queen or princess, thinking.
Woman with long hair riding indeterminate beast.
Nun, holding the martyr's wheel.
Gagged woman, clasping her hands.
Woman with a headdress, nose defaced.
Girl, right side of face scratched, scarred, nose sheared off.
Woman with hair perfectly in place, mouth and nose missing.
Crone with bottom half of face worn away, eyes staring.
Fatfaced, green woman, spewing foliage.
Young girl with floral tiara.
Woman with features erased.
Matron in bonnet and chin-piece, eyes wide, lips pursed.
Woman grinning.
Woman looking angry.
Woman's face covered with leaves, half choking.

---

[13] Previously published in Slee (2007: 35).

A litany for illiterate girls[14]

For all the ones who get sent to the fields
instead of to the school room

For the ones who carry water rather than words
who never feel the weight of learning on their heads

For the ones who try to speak up
but are always hushed up

For the ones who stay at home
while their brothers get the one chance of schooling

For the ones who put their books down
to cook the next meal
tend the sick child
walk the long mile

For the ones whose fathers say,
'What use education for her?
She will only marry and bear children.'

For the ones who try to teach themselves
and fail for lack of a teacher

For the ones who are too tired to learn
too sick, too frightened, too easily discouraged

For us who take our learning for granted
For all the books we've casually bought and placed on the shelf
                forgetting to open

---

[14]   Previously published in Slee (2007: 68).

It's a girl

The news spread like wildfire.
Sages were perplexed.
Astronomers recalculated their stars.
Shepherds sloped back to their charges.
Only the midwives smiled their knowing smiles.
And the angels crowded round,
singing 'Glory! Glory!'

Christa in the wilderness[15]

She had left some time ago.
Driven out into places of exposure
by a hunger for the solace of fierce landscapes,
she set off for abandoned wastelands on the edge of urban development,
loitered in railway sidings and along canal towpaths,
paced city rubbish tips and derelict factory sites,
walked for miles around council estates
in government-forsaken former mill towns.

No-one would think to look for her here, she thought.
Few, if any, recognised her.
Mostly, folk left her alone, sensing her taste for solitude.
Occasionally children approached, to talk
or offer stolen goods or ask for money.
Dogs, with or without owners, snapped at her heels,
looking as if they might bite.
Once, at dusk, some men high on dope bore down on her.
She carried on walking, looking ahead. They parted
like perfectly choreographed dancers, letting her go.

She walked her way along six-lane highways where the traffic
juddered and honked and slapped against her body.
She breathed in the stench of exhaust fumes,
crunched broken glass underfoot on the hard shoulder.

She had no sense of where she was going.
She wasn't going anywhere.
She needed to look on expanses that would hurt her eyes,
wouldn't offer comfort.
She needed a quality of rawness, smells that seeped into her body
and drove her on, gasping for clean air.
She didn't want trees or foliage with their promise of oasis.
She wanted absence, endlessly extending horizons,
a featureless, colourless topography
like an empty abstract canvas across which she could travel unhidden.

---

[15]   Previously published in Slee (2011: 41).

At the table of Christa[16]

The women do not serve
but are served

The children are not silent
but chatter

The menfolk do not dominate
but co-operate

The animals are not shushed away
but are welcomed

At the table of Christa

There is no seat of honour
for all are honoured

There is no etiquette
except the performance of grace

There is no dress code
except the garments of honesty

There is no fine cuisine
other than the bread of justice

At the table of Christa

There is no talk of betrayal
but only of healing and hopefulness

No money changes hands
but all know themselves rich in receiving

Death is in no-one's mind
but only the lust for life

No-one needs to command 'Remember'
for no-one present can ever forget

---

[16]   Previously published in Slee and Burns (2010: 178)

Morning tea

Sometimes I make it, sometimes it's you
in the same large blue glazed mug of Devon clay
that is to me shimmering sea, changing skies,
my grandmother's weekly wash, bluebell gleam, speedwell eye,
dream of where we might live one day.

It tastes of childhood, the farmhouse kitchen
in the early morning, my father making his solitary brew
before he goes out to feed pigs;
Methodist Sunday School rooms where country women pour
muddy rivers into rows of green cups;
rowdy family gatherings around tables boasting
pasties, varieties of cake, scones and clotted cream, trifle, buttery sponges.
Those accidents of youth: first fall off bicycle or horse;
narrow escape from the slurry pit, the time
I went flying down the school path and knocked out both front teeth;
administered then with spoonfuls of sugar by some grave-faced adult.

First thing in the morning, last thing at night,
coffee was no match – continental upstart in a jar.
No-one ever said, 'Life is patterned, regular.
Nothing so bitter it cannot be swallowed down with a little sweetness.'
Some work-muscled woman's arm simply went about its business,
filling the heavy kettle from the sink, setting it to boil on the range;
heating the pot, counting out the rich, dark stuff from the caddy,
pouring the steaming water from a height,
sniffing the vapour, setting the fat bellied pot back on the stove to brew.
The next cup of tea poured.

Envoys[17]

Death snuck into the house speaking in my mother's voice, tentative and apologetic.
The skies poured down rain all afternoon and evening, battering the doors.
Colours fled; only grey remained, draped over everything.
Later, cards tumbled through the letterbox: a flood of tenderness.
Flowers arrived unbidden, their beauty startling. The vicar came unannounced,
        carrying just
the right amount of silence, a respectful distance, good questions.

Memories I didn't realise I'd been storing up loosened themselves into my
        consciousness,
peopled my dreams. The cats, sixth senses alert, leapt on the bed, pools of warmth
against my cold flesh. Food appeared at regular intervals, on trays.
After the first day or two, taking her time, grief entered softly.
Gentle sleep poured me long potions that knocked me out for hours,
made my limbs fat and heavy as seals.

All the time, love kept pace with the envoys
arriving and leaving at strange hours of day or night.
Marked their goings and comings, opened the door for them,
tidied coats and umbrellas into the cupboard, ushered them in to see me,
made them tea or something stronger;
watched closely to ensure they did not outstay their welcome.

At the end of the first week, love locked the door, firmly bolted against further
        arrivals.
'Enough', she said, 'The house is full enough.'
We huddled down with the assorted visitors, sleeping, eating, not talking much,
whimpering occasionally, mindlessly staring out the windows,
looking after the retreating backs of cold callers,
watching the small pile of their cards gathering on the doormat.

---

[17]   Previously published in *Artemispoetry* 9 (Nov 2012), p. 11.

The river

You let the river carry you along
on its slow, unhurrying passage to the sea.

The river is composed of sunlight and moonlight,
earth's tears, and your own; mud puddles; rain
that has fallen on city roads and on mountains thousands of miles from here.

And rose petals, the pink and the white,
the flowers that are scattered on moving water at a death.

The river is composed of sorrow: the loss of a brother,
waste of a life given over to the bottle; millions
of tears he drank down, with the vodka, never shed.

Now you are shedding them for him. Crying
when the music comes, when someone speaks to you kindly.
Crying when you come home from work at night, exhausted.

The river absorbs your grief, the never to be repeated days of a life,
winks back light from every slanting angle
in which you catch sudden glimpses of

a little boy blowing out candles at a birthday party,
a visit from your brothers when you were at university,
a time you talked of Tolkien's world more real than Devon fields.

The river will turn up more as it carries you along;
from its unseen bed of stones and roots and darkness
it will bring up to its surface

leaves of last autumn, berries and fruits that the birds missed,
feathers fallen from nests, fragments of paper torn from hedgerows,
debris of a life now passed.

As you trail your fingers over the side of your small boat,
lying back with your face to an empty sky, they will catch what the river offers,
pick up each morsel, sodden and shining, examine it carefully

lay a trail along the bottom of the craft, piece leading to random piece.
Boat, woman, flotsam and jetsam, strung along a rope of river,
bearing what has to be borne, singing, weeping to the sea.

References

Angelou, Maya, *The Complete Collected Poems* (London: Virago, 1995)

Belenky, Mary Field, B.M. Clincy, N.R. Goldberger and J.M. Tarule, *Women's Ways of Knowing: The Development of Self, Voice and Mind* (New York: Basic Books, 1986)

Breeze, Jean 'Binta', *Third World Girl: Selected Poems* (Newcastle: Bloodaxe, 2011)

Butler, Judith, *Gender Trouble: Feminism and the Subversion of Identity* (New York/London: Routledge, 1990)

Chisholm, Dianne, 'Climbing like a Girl: An Exemplary Adventure in Feminist Phenomenology', *Hypatia* 23: 9–40 (2008)

Cixous, Hélène, 'The Laugh of the Medusa', *Signs: Journal of Women in Culture and Society* 1: 875–93 (1976)

Constantine, David, 'Pleasure' in *Collected Poems* (Newcastle: Bloodaxe, 2004) 326

Countryman, L. William, *The Poetic Imagination: An Anglican Spiritual Tradition* (London: DLT, 1999)

Culler, Jonathan, 'Reading as a Woman', in *On Deconstruction: Theory and Criticism after Structuralism* (London: Taylor & Francis, 1982) 43–63

Daggers, Jenny, *The British Christian Women's Movement: A Rehabilitation of Eve* (Aldershot: Ashgate, 2002)

Duffy, Carol Ann, 'Prayer', in *Selected Poems* (Harmondsworth: Penguin, 1994) 127

Duffy, Carol Ann, *The World's Wife* (London: Picador, 1999)

Furnam, Rich, Cynthia Lietz and Carol L. Langer, 'The Research Poem in International Social Work: Innovations in Qualitative Methodology', *International Journal of Qualitative Methods* 5 (3) 1–8

Gilligan, Carol, *In a Different Voice: Psychological Theory and Women's Development* (Cambridge, Mass.: Harvard University Press, 1982)

Guite, Malcolm, *Faith, Hope and Poetry: Theology and the Poetic Imagination* (Farnham: Ashgate, 2012)

Hirshfield, Jane (ed.), *Women in Praise of the Sacred: 43 Centuries of Spiritual Poetry by Women* (New York: HarperCollins, 1994)

Jantzen, Grace M., *Becoming Divine: Towards a Feminist Philosophy of Religion* (Manchester: University of Manchester Press, 1998)

Jennings, Elizabeth, *New Collected Poems* (Manchester: Carcanet, 2002)

Kamuf, Peggy, 'Writing Like a Woman' in Sally McConnell-Ginet, Ruth Borker and Nelly Furman (eds), *Women and Language in Literature and Society* (New York: Praeger, 1980), 248–99

Levertov, Denise, *New Selected Poems* (Newcastle: Bloodaxe, 2003)

Lorde, Audre, 'The Master's Tools Will Never Dismantle the Master's House', *Sister Outsider*, in *The Audre Lorde Compendium: Essays, Speeches and Journals* (London, 1996), 158–61

Lovell, Terry, 'Writing Like a Woman: A Question of Politics', in Frances Barker, Peter Hulme, Margaret Iveson and Diana Laxley (eds), *The Politics of Theory* (Essex: University of Essex, 1983)

MacLeish, Archibald, 'Ars Poetica', in *Collected Poems 1917 – 1982* (Boston: Houghton Mifflin, 1985) 106

Maitland, Sara, *A Book of Spells* (London: Michael Joseph, 1987)

Maitland, Sara, *Angel and Me: Short Stories* (London: Mowbray, 1995)

Neuberger, Julia (ed.), *The Things That Matter: An Anthology of Women's Spiritual Poetry* (London: Kyle Cathie Ltd, 1992)

Olsen, Tillie, *Silences* (New York: Delacorte, 1978)

Ostriker, Susan Alicia, *Stealing the Language: The Emergence of Women's Poetry in America* (London: Women's Press, 1987)

Prince, Ruth E.C., 'The Possibilities of an Engaged Art: An Interview with Adrienne Rich' (1998) available at http://www.english.uiuc.edu/maps/poets/m_r/rich/onlineints.htm Accessed 11.iv.13

Procter-Smith, Marjorie, *Praying With Our Eyes Open: Engendering Feminist Liturgical Prayer* (Nashville: Abingdon, 1995)

Raine, Kathleen, *Collected Poems* (Ipswich: Golgonooza, 2000)

Rich, Adrienne, *On Lies, Secrets and Silence: Selected Prose 1966–1978* (London: Virago, 1980)

Rich, Adrienne, 'Twenty One Love Poems', X111, in *The Dream of A Common Language: Poems 1974–1977* (New York/London: W.W. Norton, 1993)

Ruether, Rosemary Radford, *Sexism and God-Talk* (London: SCM, 1983)

Scholes, Robert, 'Reading Like a Man' in Alice Jardine and Paul Smith (eds), *Men in Feminism* (New York/London: Methuen, 1987) 204–18

Showalter, Elaine, 'Woman and the literary curriculum', *College English* 32: 855–62, (1971)

Sewell, Marilyn (ed.), *Cries of the Spirit: A Celebration of Women's Spirituality* (Boston: Beacon Press, 1991)

Sewell, Marilyn (ed.), *Claiming the Spirit Within* (Boston: Beacon Press, 1996)

Shuttle, Penelope, *Redgrove's Wife* (Tarset: Bloodaxe, 2006)

Slee, Nicola, 'Parables and Women's Experience', *The Modern Churchman* 26, 2 (1984) 20–31 (reproduced in Loades, A. (ed.), *Feminist Theology: A Reader* [SPCK, 1990] 41–7)

Slee, Nicola, *Praying Like a Woman* (London: SPCK, 2004a)

Slee, Nicola, *Women's Faith Development: Patterns and Processes* (Aldershot: Ashgate, 2004b)

Slee, Nicola, *The Book of Mary* (London: SPCK, 2007)

Slee, Nicola, *Seeking the Risen Christa* (London: SPCK, 2011)

Slee, Nicola and Stephen Burns (eds), *Presiding Like a Woman* (London: SPCK, 2010)

Smith, Stevie, *Collected Poems* (London: Penguin, 1975)

Soelle, Dorothee, 'Breaking the Ice of the Soul: Theology and Literature in Search of a New Language', in Sarah K. Pinnock (ed.), *The Theology of Dorothee Soelle* (Harrisburg: Trinity Press International, 2003), 31–41

Stanton, Elizabeth Cady, *The Woman's Bible* (New York: European Publishing Company, 1895, 1898)

Stein, Gertrude, *Gertrude Stein: Selected Writings* (London: Vintage, 1990)

Thorpe, Chris and Jake Lever, *Touching the Sacred: Creative Prayer Outlines for Worship and Reflection* (Norwich: Canterbury Press, 2010)

Walker, Alice, *Collected Poems: Her Blue Body Everything we Know: Earthling Poems 1965–1990* (London: Orion, 2005)

Walton, Heather, *Imagining Theology: Women, Writing and God* (London: T & T Clark, 2007a)

Walton, Heather, *Literature, Theology and Feminism* (Manchester: Manchester University Press, 2007b)

Weil, Simone, 'Reflections on the Right Use of School Studies with a View to the Love of God', in *Waiting on God* (London: Collins Fountain, 1977) 66–76

Young, Iris Marion, 'Throwing Like a Girl: A Phenomenology of Feminine Body Comportment Mobility and Spatiality', *Human Studies* 3: 137–56 (1980)

Zagajewski, Adam (2001), 'Try to Praise the Mutilated World', *New Yorker* September 24 2001, at http://www.newyorker.com/archive/2003/09/15/030915 on_onlineonly03

Zundel, Veronica (ed.), *Faith in Her Words: Six Centuries of Women's Poetry* (Oxford: Lion, 1991)

Chapter 2

Steady until Sundown: Searching for the Holy

Ruth Shelton

Searching for the Holy

A young man nervously polished his glasses and climbed onto an upended fruit crate. He began to read, hesitantly and in a low voice, to about 150 people who were laughing, drinking from buckets of red wine and taking no notice. As the reading continued, his voice became stronger and one by one people fell silent (although some accounts describe Jack Kerouac thumping the wine bucket in time with the increasing rhythm of the poem): 'The world is holy! The soul is holy! The skin is holy! The nose is holy! ... Everything is holy! Everybody's holy! Everywhere is holy!' (Ginsberg, 1984: 3–5).

'In all our memories no-one had been so outspoken in poetry before', Michael McClure remembered:

> We had gone beyond a point of no return – and we were ready for it, for a point
> of no return. None of us wanted to go back to the gray, chill, militaristic silence,
> to the intellectual void – to the land without poetry – to the spiritual drabness.
> We wanted to make it new and we wanted to invent it and the process of it. We
> wanted voice and we wanted vision. (1994: 13)

Allen Ginsberg's long poem, 'Howl', illuminates the theme of the divine in the everyday world in a country he perceives as unholy, America. His audience, in 1955, thirsty for meaning, in despair at the political rhetoric of war and threat of bombs, recognised something in his words which spoke to them and yet pointed beyond them.

In a tribute to the poet Michael Donaghy the poet Sean O'Brien writes:

> For him – as it surely should be for us – the poetry that matters, that deserves to live, that engages the imagination and nourishes the memory, emerges in contact with 'a live tradition'. It offers itself to a general audience as both challenge and invitation, to create a space which can be colonized neither by vulgarity nor remote self-regard. It is, in the teeth of the odds, poetry undertaken as an act of good faith. (2008)

In embarking on this project with the other Diviners I had little idea where it was going to lead me. I did not want to examine too closely how the (for me) implicit and given connectedness between the life of faith and the life of a poem happens. If that has been illuminated for myself and for some readers, it remains of less interest to me than an exploration of how writing poetry can take one outwards beyond limitations of culture, class and location towards the 'other' – by which I do not mean necessarily other worldly, but the world of the other person – and to meaning which has not been merely self-generated. In this chapter I will attempt to explore how the practice of faith and spirituality and the writing of poetry can be an activity in the world which effects change in oneself and others and which illuminates everyday life. I will also try to identify the barriers which prevent us continuing that journey 'in good faith'.

Those who heard Allen Ginsberg read 'Howl' experienced something unexpected, perhaps a moment when the sacred entered their lives, a moment which was intense and revelatory. Ginsberg's 'act of good faith' arguably generated other acts of good faith in his audience. Some of those might have taken the form of a conscious decision, small or large, which would affect the rest of their lives; others might have taken the form of a slight shift of consciousness of which they were barely aware.

I remember learning off by heart as a child that prayer was 'a raising of the mind and heart to God' (*Catechism of the Catholic Church*, 2000: 2559: 544). I also knew the answer to the question from the old 'Penny Catechism' 'What is a sacrament'? 'A sacrament is an outward sign of inward grace ...' The 'new' *Catechism of the Catholic*

Church describes the sacraments as 'actions of the Holy Spirit' (2000: 1116: 256) and I would now attempt to include in my understanding something about the 'act of good faith' which writing a poem, saying a prayer or receiving the Eucharist requires, being defined by its capacity to make something happen.

It is possible to propose that the common task of both the poet and the seeker of the holy is to foster a quality of attentiveness and an active readiness to see their location with new eyes and to encounter the divine in its places and people. While secular poets might reject this terminology, I have often thought that if there was a wider understanding of metaphor, there would be less division between believers and non-believers.

The authorial 'I' is highly problematic since a poem is a supremely individual act, and cannot be on behalf of anyone else, and yet it will fail if it is only about the poet. The same would be true of a prayer group leader or preacher. The writing of this chapter is, for me, a good example of the tension between the moral dimension of the responsibility involved in writing and the flawed 'I' character who fails to do any of the things that he or she points to in their writing.

Changing TV channels one day, many years ago, I found myself unexpectedly drawn to the sight of an outdoor liturgical procession. Priests, choir boys and acolytes in white robes were followed by an elderly bishop carrying a monstrance. His hands, peeping from beneath the folds of the cope, were encased in white gloves. Temporarily, I felt very moved by the hieratic reverence of the scene, which brought back vivid memories of the processions we used to take part in during my Catholic childhood. Later on in the programme, one of the priests, part of a group who had broken away from Rome over the reforms of Vatican II, was interviewed. As he spoke he became angry and looked a little mad as he condemned divorced people, gay people and non-Catholics. His emotional incontinence was in extreme contrast to the discipline observed in the presence of the sacrament. As the rant continued, my emotional response to the white gloves drained away.

A more recent television programme followed the progress of six young artists competing for the patronage of Charles Saatchi. One young woman had found a large tree trunk impaled at a dynamic angle on some London railings which she had persuaded the owners to give away. We watched men in overalls with goggles and oxyacetylene torches hack off the whole thing, tree and railings. When the piece arrived at the gallery it was carried in by men in overalls wearing white gloves. Somewhere on the journey, the trunk and railings had become art.

The artwork was too valuable in monetary terms to be handled by bare hands and the host is regarded by the institution to be too holy to be touched; even the vessel that houses the host must be kept apart. Since my childhood days, uncritically infused with the mysterious beauty of the liturgy, I have become aware that the dispensing of grace has been seized by the institution of the Church and severed from the everyday, so that it can be used as a weapon of power and control, as in the exclusion of divorced Catholics from communion. The world 'howls' because the imaginative force is crushed into submission.

Both stories reveal our human capacity for awe, wonder and reverence, but also our fear: as soon as we recognise the holy we try to control it. In the case of the artwork we assign it a commercial value: the higher the price, the more it is revered. We make rules about who can give and receive the Eucharist. The Gospels tell a story of Jesus having a meal with his friends. He broke the bread, a simple action with an everyday commodity. The immense significance, beauty and depth of the action depend upon it being an everyday event. The partakers of the bread were ordinary flawed human beings. Why, then, did this story become refined to the point that we are not allowed to touch the bread, not allowed to touch the flesh of the God who entered a womb in order to become flesh? Our attempts to apprehend the largeness and otherness of these aspects of human experience seem to make them smaller. At the same time we cannot pay attention to the everyday because we are 'gazing upwards':

> O fat white woman whom nobody loves
> Why do you walk through the fields in gloves ...
> Missing so much and so much?

Frances Cornford's poem, 'Lines on a Lady seen from a Train' (1910: 20), sounds misogynistic to present-day ears but her invective betrays an underlying anger which is nothing to do with the caricature of the woman. (G.K. Chesterton responded to the poem's cruelty with a spoof: 'The Fat White Woman Speaks' [1933: 39]: 'Why do you flash through the flowery meads, / Fat-head poet that nobody reads?' – a prescient insult, as it turned out). The poem could be, at its best, about writing and the frustration of the poet at the distancing effect of the chosen word upon the remembered experience.

If we are gloved we cannot feel, touch or remember. If we are gloved we are 'out of touch' with everyday experience. We can only search for the holy with outstretched naked hands and arms. My title 'Steady until Sundown' comes from the story of Moses (Exodus 17: 8–13) whose outstretched arms were held up by his companions as he wearied and his arms began to droop. We cannot pay attention to the world on our own.

When the invocation and proclamation of the presence of the sacred comes under the control of the institution, a shadowy spirituality, mimicking everyday experience but not grounded in it, starts to take hold and flourish. Our understanding of everyday life, having been effectively cut off from the locus of significance, is then adrift, and drained of meaning. (This is not only happening in Christian forms of spirituality, as a look through the sagging shelves of the 'Mind, Body, Spirit' section in many bookshops will demonstrate.) This kind of spirituality is very attractive, seductive even, to people struggling with pain and loss, trying to live in a competitive and alienating world where they are treated as mere economic units. A retreat, in a large house in the country, for instance, may offer space, rest, tranquil music, the potency of candles and icons to create a reflective atmosphere, and the support of others as guides or directors to help participants focus on their 'spiritual' journey. These elements may be good in themselves, but if all that is offered and experienced is escape, there is no encounter with the world and there will be no growth or change. Nothing will happen. A chasm is opened between the sacred conceived as 'wholly other' and the everyday world.

A woman walks in a garden repeating verses from a psalm: 'I cry out loud to the Lord / to the Lord I plead for mercy … You are my refuge / you are my portion / in the land of the living' (Psalms 142: 1–2). The retreat house with its open spaces is a much needed place of respite from her role as an inner city social worker, but when she repeats the words, is this a comforting reminder of the God who sustains her or a cry which comes from the depths of her day to day experience?

As a practice which is only inward, only personal and only devotional, often reflecting middle class values and aesthetics, spirituality becomes a thing in itself which, separated from everyday living and the community, can be bought and sold. In the first chapter of his book, *The Eye of the Storm*, Kenneth Leech writes:

> Today 'spirituality' is marketed as a product, in competition with others, on the
> station bookstalls. It belongs to the area of the 'private life'... Spirituality is
> widely seen not as a way of living in every sphere but as a sphere in its own right
> – 'the spiritual dimension'... It is not surprising that such spirituality serves to
> reinforce, or at least not to disturb, the status quo. (1992: 3–4)

This culture, in spirituality as in poetry, is the opposite of the 'howl' of those who are willing to risk displacement, vulnerability to the 'other', loss of status and cherished assumptions.

Outside the Church, communal respect for the idea of the sacred, which is part of the sacred itself, remains an aspect of contemporary culture. Ordinary people find ways to acknowledge aspects of life and death which touch them most deeply: lining the streets to honour war heroes, observing three-minute silences, tying flowers to lamp posts. Often these things are done in the very places, the specific locations, in which the original event happened. Inside the Church, paradoxically, it is often those who live apparently the most extreme versions of the spiritual life who offer the most grounded versions of spirituality. Philip Sheldrake quotes an American monk: 'How would you define Benedictine spirituality? We ring the bell, we recite the prayers, we live the life' (2001: 103). I remember reading an article in a Sunday supplement many years ago about Buckfast Abbey where the Abbot was quoted as saying something like 'There is a lot of nonsense talked about monastic life. Monastic life is just like any other life, it's one damn thing after another.'

Body of Work

Established artists sometimes refer to their accumulated work as their 'corpus' or 'body of work' as if they and their creations are one. I grew up with the idea that my real self existed in a bubble, encased by my body as some sort of heavy overcoat. Of course, we understood this self to be our 'soul', which in my case was a fuzzy, kidney bean shaped light, pocked with my sins or shining brightly, depending on how long it was since I had been to Confession. Poetry likewise was broadly assumed to address the soul. It was only when I began to grasp the potential totality of a poem – the sound, the texture, the infinitesimal slice of sensation that it might or might not capture – that I saw how the soul might be given permission to seep through the body, jump around it, go back in again and most importantly reveal itself in the body. A poem can go where it wills (see my poem 'Verbatim'). This was the beginning of a new understanding that I was one, integrated being. I understood it intellectually, in spite of the fact that the kidney bean-shaped light inside me is still there, a concept or an image learned so early that I have been unable to banish it. The lives of the homeless people I work with are written on their faces, their bodies desperate for food, for warmth. How can this be separate from their longing for stability and friendship? How can we offer one without offering the other?

Wittgenstein's challenge to the familiar philosophical idea of the self as distinct from the body – 'The human body is the best picture of the human soul' (1953: 178) – disrupts the idea, not only that the details of everyday life and of the body are somehow less valuable than the soul with its separate, lofty aspirations but calls those details into life as the life of the soul (or self) itself.

Calling Out

Christians from a wide range of traditions recognise and lament that spirituality and social action have become separated. Women and men, far more involved in the struggle for justice and equality than I am, speak of the limitations of a spirituality which appears to avoid and evade the demands of justice and the cause of a more equal world. These discussions often presuppose a given polarity which colludes with the argument it is opposing. Why would we need to 'bring together' concepts and activities which are one concept, one activity in the first place? In *A Theology of Liberation*, Gustavo Gutiérrez writes:

> There are not two histories, one profane and one sacred, 'juxtaposed' or 'closely linked', rather there is only one human destiny. (2001: 151)

Jesus did not lead two lives, one sacred and one secular, or preach two messages. The life that he led, the friends that he chose, the words that he spoke and the manner of his death were all of a piece, like the seamless garment.

I once undertook a two-year course in Spiritual Direction. While I learned a lot and still think with affection of the other participants, it took me many years to work out that I had always been uneasy with some of the assumptions which shaped the sessions. I felt like (and was once described as, by the course leader) the 'enfant terrible' of the group. My interventions, often on the subject of social justice, felt crude and out of place, to me as well as to the tutors. I accepted the critique from one of the leaders that my social activism was a distortion because it was not balanced with enough contemplative practice. I still accept that this may be true because reflection is an essential part of action, but the assumption underlying the critique is that social action is separate from spirituality.

I was asked at the beginning of the course to keep a journal, which didn't flourish, but towards the end of the course I wrote over 20 poems within a very short space of time. I had always written poetry, since childhood, but these poems were in a new voice and this was when I started sending poems to magazines with a view to publication. Over 16 years later, a friend has helped me see that the poems were a way of breaking through an enforced culture. They spoke in a voice that was my own but seemed to come from somewhere else, certainly not in the language of the course or much of the language of the Church. Spirituality has within itself the capacity to break out of such cultural control, just as the moment when 'Howl' broke open on the world could be described as a spiritual moment, a new way of being in the world. Spirituality disrupts power by paying attention to the unlooked for, the unseen, the marginalised and the forgotten. It is a way of 'living in every sphere', a way of displacing oneself (or preferably the community) from comfortable and self-defining places. It is the practice of living well and fully, which always takes us (often very reluctantly) outwards. The Greek word for Church, *ekklesia* (from *ek*, out, and *kaleo*, call) indicates not only that the central Christian notion of community is about being together but also that truly being together involves displacement. Henri Nouwen writes:

> In voluntary displacement community is formed, deepened and strengthened – each time we want to move back into what is ordinary and proper, each time we yearn to be settled and to feel at home we erect walls between ourselves and others, undermine community and reduce compassion to the soft part of an essentially competitive life. (1982: 64)

A friend of mine wrote to me recently, describing his arrival in Suzhou Province in China where he had gone to work as a teacher. After a very long journey from the airport during which he was handed over, at fixed points, from one unsmiling, silent individual to another, he was left at the door of his apartment in a new western-style high rise. He had no idea where he was. From the window all he could see were more of the same kind of buildings. The lampshades had cellophane wrapped around them. There was no food in the fridge. He found his way out of the building in search of 'life', as he put it. He walked through a concrete underpass and as he emerged he heard the sound of laughter. In a nameless space between the backs of the high rise blocks, local Chinese people were setting up a market. A few lychees were spread out on a handkerchief. An old woman stirred bean curd in a large bucket. Teenage boys were filleting fish and splashing each other with water. The buildings around, which previously had felt alienating and even threatening, were now the 'walls' of the impromptu market. My friend could begin slowly to make sense of his surroundings. In this account the stranger, or traveller, was able to feel at home because he was open to being at home wherever he found himself.

'Imagination is Evidence of the Divine'[1]

In my childhood the sacred was not astonishing, but a dimension of the world so utterly accepted that it did not belong to a separate sphere. The lives of the saints, particularly the more lurid details, were as real to us as if they had happened yesterday. St Francis talked to the birds so we did too. Guardian angels accompanied us and sat beside us on the school bus. St Anthony found lost things and Our Lady with her mysterious and beautiful titles, 'Tower of Ivory', 'Star of the Sea' and so on, answered our prayers and was deemed capable of travelling to earth and talking to us as she did to Bernadette at Lourdes, and Lucia, Francisco and Jacinta at Fatima.

We all wrote and read poetry at home too. We were given old diaries to write in, and I can still see my brother, now a poet, muttering under his breath while filling page after page of the diary with scribbles. At that time he was too young to read or write. I am still unsure where it came from but the sense we had of a connection between the holy and the arts, particularly poetry, has remained with

---

[1]   Words attributed to William Blake.

me. In the Catholic culture in which I grew up, image and word peaceably swapped places. I suppose we did not distinguish between a luminous 'Our Lady' who watched over us on our bedside tables, a Renaissance painting of the Madonna, or the story in Luke about her meeting with Elizabeth. What mattered was her mysterious presence in the world. Pablo Picasso is widely accredited with having said 'Everything you imagine is real'. We could make things we imagined real by writing about them or painting them, but the image on the piece of paper was not valued much more than the image in our heads. The conferring of equal status on the 'inward eye' with that of the physical world has caused me some problems in adult life! Occasionally I look back on this time with longing, but in a way it was a bit like being a pagan, all was sacred so nothing was asked of me.

In his autobiography, *Timebends*, Arthur Miller defines stupidity as 'the want of empathic power' (1987: 72). After a concert or (very occasionally) a poetry reading, people can talk easily about being 'taken out of themselves'. But taken out of themselves to where? The power of the imagination (again, a phrase which slips off our tongues too easily) can take us to where other people struggle and suffer. We are able to stand where they stand, and look at the world with their eyes. This call to action, overtly expressed, is rarely successful in a poem, but when I am writing this is adjacent to what I am attempting to do. The agitated wings of the spirit beat and churn our familiar air, creating currents which uphold us as we fly to where, perhaps, we would rather not go.

City Life

For some this might be the City. True Cockneys define themselves as being born within earshot of the Bow bells. I have never lived anywhere in Nottingham (where I was born and live now) where I could not hear the bells of the clock in the Old Market Square in the centre of the City that continues to be a vital source of material for my poems. I grew up with a given understanding of the holiness of everything, but our postmodern, pluralistic culture asks something from those who want to search for and understand what the holy is, if anything. Part of the response to this demand has been one of flight from the contemporary world and in particular the city. Yet, according to scripture, God loved the city. 'The vision of the heavenly city stands firm against the pagan Elysian fields', as Andrew Davey puts it in his essay 'Spirituality of Everyday Life' (2005: 106). The call to enter the New Jerusalem is a call to participate in its making, and to be in the presence of God. Rowan Williams speaks of this call in his sermon 'Holy Space': 'The light of presence is not the sanctuary lamp but the light in which the people of God see each other's faces' (1994: 102). The walls have come down, there is no need for churches or designated holy spaces, the whole space of the city is 'the whole common life of the redeemed community' (Williams, 1994: 102).

The influence of liberation theology in recent times has helped us to take location seriously as the contexts in which human activity takes place. Location is essential in the discourse of liberation theology for the formation of our spirituality and theology: the places where we live, work, worship and encounter others. Spirituality and theology which seem at times to be almost completely separated come together in urban areas, in which there is an organic reality to the practice of faith and the pursuit of the Kingdom's justice.

I have been on the judging panel of a few poetry competitions and any poet who has done this will tell you that the majority of poems will describe emotions which arise from being in English countryside (apart from the significant minority which are about the demise of the steam train). Some will draw on rural images and metaphors irrespective of where they live or even the subject of the poem. In the same way the shadowy spirituality, at its worst, wanders in a nameless floating landscape which is neither rural nor urban and which is devoid of warmth, sexuality or passion for justice and fears the political world as squalid and contaminating.

The Wide Awake Gaze

Walter Benjamin, one of the leading cultural theorists of the twentieth century, based his famous enquiry into the notion of the everyday in the Arcades area of Paris, an area of shopping malls in the city teeming with life, bombarding the onlooker with multi-layered images and experiences. The notion of phantasmagoria is a persistent theme throughout the work. Benjamin, in the age of magic lanterns, light shows and early photographic experiments, pointed to the dream-like state which modernity engenders and the processes which create the spectacle. In our time we might think of the crowded underground railway system ('the tube') in London as an area of experience which overwhelms, becoming phantasmagoria, moving images which we cannot process or relate to. Each person on the tube with us has a name, a life and a history but we avoid looking them in the eye because of the dream-like state that such an experience engenders. Benjamin points us, not to the dream-like state of our own lives but to the hidden processes that produce the spectacle. The study of the teeming, everyday life of the streets would bring the historian and the reader to the threshold of the present, to the point of waking. Today's life and culture, with the centrality of the image and the overwhelming demands of urban life, requires a wide-awake spirituality of which poetry could be the lens.

In *A Berlin Chronicle* Walter Benjamin urges 'the wanderer' to pay attention to the city in the same way that poets traditionally have evoked the beauty of the rural landscape:

> Then, signboards and street names, passers-by, roofs, kiosks, or bars must speak
> to the wanderer like a cracking twig under his feet in the forest, like the startling
> call of a bittern in the distance. (1986: 8–9)

The city calls out to the poet as it does to the seeker of truth and justice in a multi-layered concatenation of voices, demanding attention, perhaps love. The wave of a gloved hand is not enough.

Wide-awakeness is the presiding spirit of Adam Zagajewski's *Mysticism for Beginners*, which not only describes the everyday, but uses the everyday as a way of answering the question of what spirituality is or might be:

> The day was mild, the light was generous,
> the German on the café terrace
> held a small book on his lap.
> I caught sight of the title:
> 'Mysticism for Beginners'.
> Suddenly I understood the swallows
> patrolling the streets of Montepulciano
> with their shrill whistles,
> and the hushed talk of timid travelers
> from Eastern, so-called Central Europe, ... (1999: 7)

In the opening line of this poem the poet describes the essential conditions for the mystic gaze: 'The day was mild, the light was generous'. He looks, not rapaciously straining or seeking a higher illumination, nor colonising what he sees for some separate purpose. In his meekness he inherits the real earth on which he stands, the disclosure of the everyday. His notion of mysticism does not belong to him, it is not something he has earned but is a gift from another (the enemy?), a German on the cafe terrace. The poet does not claim the idea, central theme or title of the poem as his, but projects them onto a book lying open for everyone to read. Suddenly he 'understands' the swallows in this particular street, in this particular town, Montepulciano. In the 'generous light' their 'speech', their shrill whistles, and later the nightingale 'practicing its speech', are equally understood by him as the hushed talk of timid travellers from his own country, 'hushed' by others and renamed as Central Europe. Memories are integrated into the present; the herons, yesterday, the day before. He goes on to describe the head of a little princess that he has seen the day before in the Louvre. Art and nature equally dazzle and are infused with the same source of energy:

> and stained glass like butterfly wings
> sprinkled with pollen,
> and the little nightingale practicing
> its speech beside the highway,
> and any journey, any kind of trip,
> are only mysticism for beginners,
> the elementary course, prelude
> to a test that's been
> postponed. (1999: 7)

Finally we are brought under the poem's mild gaze and generous light. All our journeys – to work, shopping, towards and away from one another – are trips to our own lives, to the everyday. Mysticism is not some higher attainment for exceptionally gifted individuals, but a gift which we already have. The joke which ends the poem is that we cannot see our own giftedness or the giftedness in our own context, but live our lives as if we have failed some imaginary test.

Naming and Creating

'Who better to understand the nature of words than a poet?' This rash question was asked in 1955 by David Wallace, manager of marketing research for Ford's 'E-car' project (Richler, 1983: 66–73). The poet Marianne Moore was asked to contribute names for the E-car, and her list included 'Mongoose Civique', 'Andante con Moto' and 'Utopian Turtletop'. The E-car was finally christened by Ford as the Edsel.

In scripture, calling and creating are closely linked. 'He made the stars and named them one by one' (Isaiah 40: 26). Name giving, as in the stories about Jacob (Genesis 32: 22–31) and Peter (John 1: 40–42), accompanies the moment of their calling by God. During the World Cup series in 2012, I saw a street cleaner pulling his cart, the sort of person who is almost invisible, an extra in the daily drama of the streets. I only saw him because on the front of his cart an England flag fluttered, bravely. There is a poem there, although I haven't written it. But if someone were to write it, the act of writing, creating, would give the man a name, an identity, calling him out. This is not enough of course. The poem is written, the prayer is uttered but he remains poor and on the margins. However, poem and prayer continue to pay attention, a kind of homage, and slowly the power of the Word will do what it must do: transform the shape of the world that we carry in our minds and imaginations, a shape which, otherwise, is almost always made in our own image.

In the story of Jesus and the rich young man (Mark 10: 21), Jesus looks at him and loves him. The way he looks at him – *emblepsas* – is variously translated as 'affectionately' or 'steadily' or the quality of his gaze encapsulated in 'beholding him'. I prefer 'steadily' to convey a quality of attention which calls its subject into being and life. Jesus loved the young man even though he was, like us, incapable of doing what Jesus asked of him. 'Go, sell everything you have, and give it to the poor ... then come and follow me' (Mark 10: 21–2). Jesus and the young man stood there, on the real ground of their lives, each longing for the other, and wishing that things were different.

A poem, like our longing for God, is pitched between lack and desire, as we wrestle with systemic contradictions, writing into our world the details, the touch, how we wish things to be, the act of creation marked on our (and we hope, our readers') consciousness. This struggle for transformation would be recognised by anyone reading the Gospels, but it is a struggle which can only be engaged in with bare hands and unguarded hearts, not white gloves and robes of office (of whatever sort).

Encountering the Word

Among the poems selected for this book, four of them – 'I Asked a Man for a Light', 'Gallagher's Way', 'The Order of Brightness' and 'When Pigeons Fall' – are poems from a collection I have been working on for a number of years, on and off, loosely connected to the Arthurian myths. The 'I' figure in this series is highly problematic since the voice can only have come from me and it would be presumptuous to assume that I could speak on behalf of anyone else. The device of the voice, however, allows me to imagine another self, and wander about in their imaginary landscape. The collection concerns a central character called Arthur, who might or might not be homeless, who might or might not be the Arthur of the myths, and who might or might not be a king. The final lines from David Jones' poem, 'The Sleeping Lord', had been in my head for a long time:

> Does the land wait the sleeping lord
> > or is the wasted land
> that very lord who sleeps? (1974: 96)

The idea continued to develop very slowly when I began work in the mid-seventies in a day centre for homeless people, Emmanuel House in Nottingham. During that time the founder and director of the project, Fr Roger Killeen, became a good friend and mentor. He told me stories of growing up in Ireland where the 'gentlemen of the road' marked the doorways of houses where they had been made welcome with chalk. He often recalled how his mother would ask Roger and his brothers and sisters to bring the visitor into the kitchen and make the required tea and sandwiches. Not only that: the children were told to call the visitor 'sir'. These memories inspired him to found Emmanuel House.

In those days the old street drinkers would sit in circles in inner city parks to share the day's bottles. These 'schools' were governed by unwritten and arcane but fiercely defended rules; whoever was 'paid' that day bought the bottle. If they didn't, the sanctions could be savage. The 'Sir Tramps' of Roger's recollection and these quixotic but governed circles, their 'high' language of drama and catharsis, the sudden and immediately acted-on impulses or quests, conflated in my mind with the Arthurian legends. It seemed that in themselves 'the knights of the road', the itinerant, homeless citizens of the city were signifiers, their gestures, tics, habits and speech were prophetic wonders and signs of the times.

Many of the Arthur poems explore themes around silence and voicelessness. In the contemporary world, true physical silence is hard to find and seems to make people feel uncomfortable. At the same time, many people are marginalised because their voices are not heard. The permanent noise is a kind of silence, a state of not hearing the cry of people living on the margins.

For many years I held writing classes in HMP Nottingham and other prisons. One way of engaging the participants was through song lyrics, because they all listened to the radio. Among the main differences between poetry and song lyrics is that poetry can be read in silence and depends on silence as part of its structure whereas a song is designed only to be heard. Some of the participants in the writing groups found this difficult, cramming the rhythm and metre, and experiencing space as unsatisfactory, even intolerable. I felt that there might be a connection between this anxiety and their circumstances – a connection between the gaps and silences that surround a poem and the unheard men and women of the cities whose stories are made up for them by others. Silence in poetry created by caesurae, the margins, between the lines, and at the end of a poem, contains its own power in which everyone can articulate their own narrative, or just let the silence speak for them. The unheard silence of the city is a dimension of my poem, 'I Asked a Man for a Light'.

Two other poems, 'Prime Time' and 'Breaking News', are selected from poems I have sent out each year instead of a Christmas card. 'How to Make a Scene' was the poem for Christmas 2012 and reflects some of the autobiographical material which was required for this chapter. Each year, people are kind enough to respond to these poems, ask questions and even contact me before Christmas to ask what the theme is going to be. It seems that, as I explore images and metaphors about the Incarnation, popular ideas and legends around the birth of Jesus, and my own understanding of the stories, the recipients of the poems are exploring with me, so that it becomes a live exchange and a mutual greeting. In some odd way, because the poems are written for people I know, there is a sense of continuity between each one, even though they are written a year apart. The awareness of the listener creates a semantic community of 'surround sound' which reverberates back and forth, sometimes changing or adding to the meaning, or divining meaning of which the poet is unaware. Philosophers speak of 'performative utterances' where to speak is to act, and that act effects permanent change. 'I name this ship' is a common example. Between reader and poet, as between the pray-er and the prayed for, there is a mysterious common activity in which things are changed forever.

My poem, 'Transport', in part draws on a favourite film 'Wings of Desire' (*Der Himmel über Berlin*, translated literally as 'The Heavens over Berlin'), a 1987 Franco-German production directed by Wim Wenders. I include a sudden shout of 'Terra del Fuego' on the London underground by way of tribute. In the film, two angels, Cassiel and Damiel, walk unseen alongside the citizens of Berlin: a pregnant woman in an ambulance on the way to the hospital, a painter struggling to find inspiration, a broken man who thinks his girlfriend no longer loves him. Through their dialogue we learn of their task, to witness the development in humanity of 'spirit'. In this extract, Cassiel and Damiel are sitting side by side in a car which is for sale in a car showroom. Cassiel takes out his notebook and begins to read his regular report out loud.

> CASSIEL: And today, on the Lilienthaler Chaussee, a man, walking, slowed down, and looked over his shoulder into space. At Post Office 44, a man who wants to end it all today pasted rare stamps on his farewell letters, a different one on each. He spoke English with an American soldier – the first time since his schooldays – and fluently. A prisoner at Plotzenzee, just before ramming his head against the wall, said: 'Now!' At the Zoo U-Bahn station, instead of the station's name, the conductor suddenly shouted: 'Tierra del Fuego!'
> DAMIEL: Nice.

I love the demotic 'Nice' at the end of the dialogue. The angels interpret 'spirit' by paying attention, by reverencing everyday details. When Damiel falls in love with a trapeze artist (her costume includes a pair of wings) he chooses to leave heaven to be with her. When he 'lands' he goes to a café. To taste, to bleed, to feel – the culmination of his centuries-long wish for physicality – is concentrated on the blissful experience of drinking a cup of coffee and smoking a cigarette. Poets have something to learn from Damiel's return to earth. As an angel he looks dramatic and noble in a long black coat. Once on earth he buys a cheap leather jacket and ill-fitting trousers and shoes. His immersion into reality is not aesthetically satisfying – his appearance jars, his walk is ungainly. His is the beauty of the everyday, calling forth our empathy, our bewilderment and our distaste, in a way that he never could, as an angel.

'From The 110th Floor' was inspired by the work of Michel de Certeau (1925–1986), the French Jesuit and scholar whose chapter 'Walking in the City' (1988: 156ff) was based on his observations from the top of the World Trade Centre in New York, a poignant standpoint from our perspective. He observed that through walking in the city, people created their own style, their own pathways, a sort of language which spoke about the city and contributed to creating its meaning. The pedestrian gives new meanings to places and streets which are not the same as those originally assigned to them. The purposeful cat in 'Swedenborg's Drains' also represents the transgressive imagination, making pathways to new, or other worlds.

As a way of exploring these ideas I decided to write a poem ('There Will Be No More Temples in the City') which was constructed by recording every piece of writing: billboard, graffiti, 'Back Soon' notes, personalised wheelie bins, every consciously scripted mark on the face of the city in a specific location, in this case one side (it's a long road!) of the Radford Road in inner city Nottingham. I made many discoveries during this project. For instance, although it is among the highest recorded areas of deprivation nationally as well as locally, there are many businesses and small enterprises there. There are very few graffiti, but the occasional flourish is highly stylised and not abusive. Notices, flyers, hoardings and shop fronts disclose food, celebration and travel as major preoccupations. Although I live near this street, in many ways I am a tourist there but I would rather not be. Tourism brings you back home unchanged. In an encounter, you are changed forever and you never quite go back home. A poem should have the quality of an encounter for poet and reader, both responding to the echoing mysteriousness happening in the space between.

Cracks in the Concrete

'If I read a book and it makes my whole body so cold no fire can ever warm me, I know that is poetry' (Dickinson in Johnson 1958: 472–4). It is hard to imagine the reclusive Emily Dickinson on the London tube, but her famous remark reminds me of a phrase (attributed, among others, to Herman Melville writing about Hawthorne) now used widely to describe the power of literature to raise one's level of awareness above its own capacity: 'the shock of recognition'. This recognition which poetry is capable of engendering may be one last vestige of connection with our selves. In 2007, feeling exhausted after a long interview for a job I knew I hadn't got, I went to Tate Modern to see 'Shibboleth' in the Turbine Hall by the Colombian sculptor Doris Salcedo. I still cannot think of this piece without associating it with the 'shock of recognition'. It ran the full 167 metres (548 feet) of the cavernous hall, beginning as a hairline crack in the concrete floor of the building, then widening and deepening as it snaked across the room. There was some mystery as to how it was 'installed' (a mystery no doubt carefully managed by the Tate marketing department) and the vestiges of it, if you look closely, are still there. 'The Crack' (as I think of it) both described and illuminated the everyday and any 'beyondness' which it evoked was present in its own physicality. At the time I attributed the astonishing impact of the work at least partly to my own exhaustion. Much later in Philip Wander's introduction to Henri Lefebvre's *Everyday Life in the Modern World* I read:

> But beyond the bleakness of an everyday life regulated by the needs of consumption, Lefebvre points to 'the cracks in the concrete' made by that which cannot be wholly repressed; the awakening of sexual desire and love; the undeniable delights of play; and the allure of the festival; the bursting of work time and pre-fabricated leisure experience into celebration. (Lefebvre 2000 p ix)

The everyday is also dangerous because, as Henri Lefebvre notes: 'it exposes the possibilities of conflict between the rational and the irrational in our society and our time' (2000: 23). It is the nature of poetry to be dangerous, to burst through the cracks, to surprise, to invert, to praise, to illuminate: a list of activities which sounds very much like the job description of the Holy Spirit.

The crack in the Turbine Hall was surrounded by Health and Safety warnings because it was, in places, several inches deep. These warnings were apposite because the everyday is open-eyed towards the exercise of power.

Christine Levich's translation of Henri Lefebvre reads:

> Banality? Why should the study of the banal be itself banal? Are not the surreal, the extraordinary, the surprising, even the magical, also part of the real? Why wouldn't the concept of everydayness reveal the extraordinary in the ordinary? (1987: 9)

A few years ago I was in the back of a taxi and the driver and I both noticed a man lurching painfully down the road towards the city centre. I knew this man vaguely, although he never appeared in any of the day centres or hostels. His progress, as his body swung dangerously from side to side on two sticks, was so slow that often I passed him going into town and, on my return, he would still be making his way down the hill. With every excruciating lurch forward he emitted a loud groan. The taxi driver said to me: 'We have people like that in my country' (which turned out to be Nepal); 'they are holy men.' And turning round to face me, hands still on the wheel, with a smile he said, 'I think he turns clay into gold'.

When Pigeons Fall[2]

… and then I sat on the steps of the Council House
between the stone lions who seem
to be guarding something, I don't know what;
Hint of marble within, uniforms,
do they not know that I am a king?
That day I asked questions of the air, the pigeons
and these are my questions: when I look at my hand
who am I looking at? When pigeons fall
from the sky, why are the cracks
smoothed over, made blue again?
The orange flags, stirring above cars in Motor Mart,
what country? What song are they singing?
and this drum drum beat beat which says do this do that
every day, hearing it. I know I've left my sword somewhere;
spurs, fealty, quest, words people heard and answered
all tumbled by the side of the road.
No-one, not even my Key Worker, who has the answer
to everything in her filing cabinet, can answer these questions.
Why does the fountain seem triumphant and why can I recognize the joy
when I can't remember it? What do I sound like when I speak
and most of all where among the pigeons is the one who cries 'you, you'?
When will the doorways pour light
onto my waiting head?

---

[2]   Commended as runner-up in Manchester Cathedral International Religious Poetry Competition 2012.

I Asked a Man for a Light

I asked a man for a light, once,
and he gave it to me. Car lights
swam in the rain; cars hooted,
the bricks of the Night Shelter
red, black, blue, red, black,
blue, as clubbers parted around us.
I have this one rule, I call none of them
Sir. This one's face
bending towards me, was ordinary,
darkish, he'd cut himself shaving;
circles under his eyes.
It wasn't a great moment for me
I try to avoid this sort of thing,
and for him it would be forgotten
before it was over. If it were not
that he looked tired, and his lighter
was square and polished,
dark hairs on his thumb
rain on his lapel,
and that, briefly, in the flame,
he looked at me,
I would have forgotten it myself.

Gallagher's Way

'He has the way of it,' said Smudge,
we nodded, drained our glasses,
conjuring Gallagher and his way,
walking everywhere, upturned eyes
seeming sightless; (he could see alright)
fixed on something floating above his head.
'A bottle most likely,' said Binky,
or a cup, I said. But we all agreed
that Gallagher has the way of it.

Every day he meets a swan
in the stone lake behind the Museum.
Every day the swan comes looking
importantly, like a witness at a line-up,
then rearing, in a blink half-snake,
the black line of his face breaking,
Gallagher holding his one piece of bread
over the warning 'Do Not Feed
These swans can be dangerous'.

'He drinks the same way,' said Chalky.
'Gazing above the glass for a minute
before raising the next.' The way
he buttons his coat precisely,
tied round the middle with a striped necktie,
one hand pressed on his breast pocket
where the bread is, treading steadily,
those upturned eyes unchanging,
never wavering or stumbling.

'He'll be in, in a minute,' said Smudge,
and we fell quiet, looking at the chair
as if waiting for something to begin.
'Did y'ever see him fall?' asked Binky.
'He'll fall down finally,' said Chalky,
'when he's had enough, still in his coat'
'With those eyes, you'd not know the difference,'
said Tully, who'd had a few, but old Mary
said, 'I'd like a little piece of that bread from him, myself.'

Remembering Earl[3]

1 small cabbage, 1lb pots, 1pkt. streaky (if cheap).
Rosary at 8. Write to Earl.
The butter sputters in my bent pan
Smearing Norah's postcard of the Bridge of Sighs,
which I'd always imagined as puffs of breath,
like broken beads,
barely holding their own.

Our breaths froze in the dark mornings,
as we carried cabbage and bacon to the boys.
That pearl of air was part of me,
but where's it gone? 'You have some fancies,' says Norah
She thinks I'm simple, writing to Death Row
but it's not easy. 'Just be yourself,'
the lady from Amnesty said.

During the Sorrowfuls I saw his black finger
tracing my writing on the airmail paper.
During the Joyfuls (which Norah gabbles)
I saw the rare light, like a medal on his breastbone.
During the Glorious Mysteries, his breath rose
from behind the walls like a long-held note.
his whole lost body failing to come out.

---

[3]   Commended as runner-up in Manchester Cathedral International Religious Poetry
Competition 2011.

Prime Time

Beside a boarded-up Burger King,
a white pigeon began to sing.

In the aisles of 'Everything's a Pound'
two enemies passed – then turned around.

While Krista slept in the bus station,
forgotten stars made a new constellation,

and midnight chimed. Sleepers in the doorways heard
their names, and as they stirred

The Town Hall's stone lions spread their wings,
three homeless men appeared as kings,

and a sail unfurled in the waiting skip
which cleaved through The Square as a blazing ship,

a child at the helm. Women of the night wrote on the prow
'We name this ship the Here and Now.'

Transport

Late one afternoon, on the Piccadilly line
between Knightsbridge and Acton, where once
I'm told, the Jarrow hunger marchers sat
in a terraced street, and the women ran out with food
and the marchers sang 'Jerusalem'
by way of thanks and rose up again, silently,
and a man with an eye-patch
sitting next to me said suddenly, very loudly;
'Tierra del Fuego! Tierra del Fuego!'
A woman in a knitted beret with a thistle hatpin
was reading a typed manuscript, open on her knee,
'Wild plants of the London Underground'.
With each shudder of the train she mouthed
'Squirrel-tail fescue, Fool's watercress,
Mouse-ear hawkweed, Yarrow.'
The train shook over a narrow bridge
and I could see a row of houses with yellow doors
and a woman taking pyjamas, sheets, towels, off the line
and when the person on the other side of me got off
at Barons Court they left behind a half-open bag
and a clown costume was spilling out,
a false nose on elastic and some shiny cloth
with pompoms. I picked it up
with some idea of doing something – what?
and I wondered if someone had been a clown
and changed their mind, there and then,
wanting to be someone else, and was at that moment,
sitting on one of those wooden benches on the platform
with the station name along the back on enamelled metal panels
which are a unique feature on the entire London Underground.

The Order of Brightness

Each Christmas they make an arch of stars
in the precinct, spelling out
'Festive Bonanza – Doug's Used Cars',
but I haven't noticed.

'Do not sit here' warns the arrow,
pointing to the blue-glazed steps – this is the place,
beneath the blank eye of the disappearing sparrow
on the 'Birds of Britain' mural.

My bags look up at me like children
and I begin. I don't need their shreds of paper,
just their fat shapes and rapt attention.
Stars shoot and return.

Wilfrid – cause of death unknown,
James 'Binky' O'Neil – the winter,
Seamus – an infected splinter,
Patsy – just decided time to go.
The Weasel, loathed by all, disappeared.
Also Feegan with his Assyrian beard,
Whisky John.
Geordie 'The Crow' set on fire
Meredith, climbing St. Aidan's Spire,
Blind Mary, the winter.
Officer, I'm halfway through,
Sir Fingers Donnelly – adieu,
Queenie missed her step.

Let go of my arm, I've done.
You rolling shutters, rattle. Stars
flow down, prick through my overcoat.
Your names are the pain in my bones.

How to Make a Scene

Up-end a cardboard box, paint it brown and green,
paste red cellophane behind the cut-out window,
light a candle (ask a grown-up to help),
run round; be awed, astonished at the glow;

find Mexican Mary in her brown poncho.
Noah will do for Joseph from the old Noah's ark.
Twice his size, a raffia sheep keeps watch
with an odd menagerie; one year, a clock-work shark.

Leave them round the empty walnut shell, the half-dark
is alive with expectation; it will follow you up the stairs
and never leave you. Somewhere on the journey
the Town Hall clock strikes midnight: you are there

under the Christmas lights in the Market Square.
You speak, she doesn't answer, there's nothing you can say,
she smiles back and pats her belly,
you stay a while, give money, turn away.

Turn back. Walk towards the woman and her child,
crouch beside them to keep dry.
Peer round the cardboard,
at the rare worshipper,
the passers by.

Swedenborg's Drains

On this spot, which you know
well, at the bottom of my street,
where it joins the boulevard and the park,
where each year there is a fair,
where tree roots swell
through the paving-stones,
we parted. 'See you next week!'
As we say it, we see it, heads bent
over the table, but I have to go,
the drain men are there
with their rods and cameras.
Next door's cat with exact feet leads
me to the screen they've set up
in my back yard. Inside
an engraved page flutters
open, Emmanuel signals
to William, their effortless angels
stir underground. 'Have a look,'
says the drain man. The cat brushes
against blue tunnels, parallel rooms,
where you and I are still
at the bottom of the street,
roots growing from our soles.

Verbatim

I'm hiding a gift, one hand behind my back.
Behind us the sky changes, blue, grey, blue grey,
disappearing on the lips like sugar, lightening
above the staggered satellite dishes, transmitters, observation towers.
Now we can see the rain. I wish I were not consoled by this,
I wish I were consoled by the emblazoned ARISE on the end terrace wall.
I wish I were the busker's fanfare; here I come,
struggling through the entrails of his trombone,
landing upside down, seeing what he sees, the streets, the pouring light,
Oh yes, the gift. I've opened my hand, it's empty.
Take it. If you do, all that's gone before
will never be the same again.

From the 110th Floor

Pitched between twin and twin, the endless
thin skin of sky, he watched, uncertain, always
of the unseen, tugging like tides

between

the grid of West Side Highway and Vesey St,
silent traffic; the angled yellow cabs,

packed like bees. He repeated notions
from unfinished chapters; consolations and desolations
as familiar as his own circulating

blood, rushed up

one tower, down the next, blending as they always
would, into one. '*It's hard to be up when you're down*'

'Must one descend fall back finally into
the dark space where crowds move back and forth…?'
– On the other hand, they are in the arms of lovers –

a fall of grace

He extended his fused fingers, the wing
of his body covered the pigeons, their stratagems.

There will be No More Temples in the City

with verses from the book of Ezekiel, chapters 40–43

At the beginning of the year, on the tenth day of the month, in the twenty-fifth year of our exile.
tell us everything you see

Mann Leisure, Sale and Distribution of Amusement Machines, also TV and video repairs; Midlands Community Training and Development (boarded up), The Sanctuary.

The length of the rod which the man was holding was six cubits.

Nations Grid Gas (defended by steel fence) Pound£leshcontempt appearing, Dovetail Joinery manufacturer of Exclusive and Fitted Furniture, Whatever You're Planning for in 2012 We Can Help.

Reckoning by the long cubit which was one cubit and one hand's breadth.

5 star Motors – Car washing incl. Sundays, also Parts, Keep Hyson Green Blooming, Jesus4Shariah. Chapatti Junction Curry King, Warszawa International Mini Market, Persian Mini-Market, mind the step.

He measured the thickness and height of one wall, each was one rod.

Ozi's £ Plus, Demad House Lace Manufacturers. (on a wheelie-bin) 'All the darkness cannot put the light out of a candle' Patik loves Rosie. Kerkuk Restaurant – men only, (on a wheelie-bin) Knowledge without Understanding is Empty.

He measured the threshold of the gateway, each depth was one rod. Each cell was one rod long, and one rod wide, and there was a space of five cubits between the cells

Faith in Action: Enjoy the Fun – Party Games, Please drop your washing off here. Bro, where was ya, I waited 2 hours, Adult Shop. E-**L**-evate School of Motoring, Win your golden ticket here!

The threshold of the gateway on the side facing the temple was one rod.

Mishimushi Records, Church of the Body of Christ Car Park , Youth for Christ Night Tonight.

Now the cells of the gateway, looking back eastwards, were three in number on each side, all of them same size, and their pilasters on either side were each of the same size

Nutan Jewellers Pawnbrokers – We cash cheques – any cheque considered, The Old General – quiz night most nights, Wilok's International Food Stores – African and Caribbean Food – Mobile Phone top-ups – Money Transfers and International Calls. Drongos for Europe tickets here.

He measured the entrance to the gateway; it was ten cubits wide, and the width of the gateway itself was thirteen cubits

Christelle Shop African Hair and Beauty Design. Back in 10. Final Cut – Men's Hair designs, open 'til midnight. Madni Sweet Mart and Pan House, Karczna Pod Zbóbnem.

In front of the cells on each side lay a kerb, one cubit wide; each cell was six cubits by six

Accra Central Market – African-Caribbean Foods – exotic and European foods – deals in Ghanaian dishes, Hafiz Supermarket and Halal meat and Poultry, Iberian Delights delicious Panini, Cost of Botched Police Raids – your Evening Post sold here. Nadia, callers welcome, I am George, a blue-green Macaw with orange shoulders, very worried.

The man brought me to the outer court and I saw rooms and a pavement round the court. The pavement ran up to the side of the gateways, as wide as they were long

Skype calls here, Diamond Island – 7p to Ghana. Umani Fashions. All night Market – fresh fruit and vegetables daily – Fresh Naan – Charcoal oven. Carlton, I love you, if you read this you'd know.

Breaking News

A man walks alone in a field of stones,
cutting his feet on ancient stains,
Crow cries 'seed' in the leafless skies
'Bread is breaking where each stone lies.'

Ox stood by a woman and her child;
breathe-in-strength and breathe-out shield;
Ass coughs 'Fool can't do, can't do,
but my breaking back will carry you.'

Cracked bowl, empty well,
she parts dry lips but there's nothing to tell.
Rough Ground listened but Camel spoke first
'Waters are breaking for all who thirst.'

Pigeon spoke from the gargoyle's mouth,
'grain of truth, grain of truth'.
Woman of the night croons 'I love you true.'
'Yes, tonight I've come to be with you.'

References

Benjamin, Walter, *Reflections: Essays, Aphorisms, Autobiographical Writings* (New York: Schocken, 1986)

Catechism of the Catholic Church (London: Burns and Oates, 2000)

Chesterton, G.K., *Collected Poems* (London: Methuen 1933)

Cornford, Frances, *Poems* (Hampstead: Priory Press, 1910)

Davey, Andrew, 'Spirituality of Everyday Life' in *Spirituality in the City* (London: SPCK, 2005)

De Certeau, Michel, *The Practice of Everyday Life* (ET Berkeley: University of California Press, 1988)

Ginsberg, Allen, *Collected Poems 1947–1980* (New York: Harper and Row, 1984)

Gutiérrez, Gustavo A., *Theology of Liberation* (London: SCM Press, 2001)

Johnson, Thomas H. (ed.), *The Letters of Emily Dickinson, Volume 2*, (Cambridge, MA: Belknap Press of Harvard University Press, 1958)

Jones, David, *The Sleeping Lord and Other Fragments* (London: Faber & Faber, 1974)

Leech, Kenneth, *The Eye of the Storm, Spiritual Resources for the Pursuit of Justice* (London: DLT, 1992)

Lefebvre, Henri, *Everyday Life in the Modern World* (London: The Athlone Press, 2000)

Lefebvre, Henri, trans. Levich, Christine, 'Every day and Everydayness' in *Yale French Studies*, 73, Everyday Life (1987) available at http://www.andrew.cmu.edu/user/skey/research_prev/reading/The%20everyday%20and%20everydayness_Lefebvre.pdf Accessed 18 April 2013

McClure, Michael, *Scratching the Beat Surface* (New York: Penguin, 1984)

Miller, Arthur, *Timebends* (London: Methuen, 1987)

Nouwen, Henri J.M., Donald P. McNeill and Douglas A. Morrison, *Compassion* (London: DLT, 1982)

O'Brien, Sean, *On Michael Donaghy: Black Ice, Rain and the City of God*, The T.S. Eliot Lecture delivered by Sean O'Brien at the Poetry International Festival, South Bank Centre, London, on Sunday 26 October 2008 available at http://greatamericanpoetryshow.com/articles-and-essays/michael-donaghy-by-sean-obrien/ Accessed 18 April 2013

Richler, Mordecai, *The Best of Modern Humour* (New York: Knopf, 1983)

Sheldrake, Philip, *Spaces for the Sacred* (London: SCM Press, 2001)

Williams, Rowan, *Open to Judgement* (London: DLT, 1994)

Wittgenstein, Ludwig, trans. G.E.M. Anscombe, *Philosophical Investigations II*, (New York: MacMillan, 1953)

Zagajewski, Adam, trans. Clare Cavanagh, *Mysticism for Beginners* (New York: Farrar Straus Giroux, 1999)

Chapter 3

Taking Form: On Becoming a Christian Poet

Mark Pryce

Caedmon's Calling as a Poet

The earliest poem in the English language is Caedmon's *Hymn*. Bede's story of Caedmon's formation as a poet tells of how he was a herdsman in St Hilda's great abbey at Whitby – a distinguished community of poetry and song as well as religion and learning. Caedmon felt he had no skill in composing or performing, and he would hide away in the stables at night when his turn to contribute to the artistic entertainment of the place was close. One night an angel visited him in the hay: 'Caedmon, compose!' 'I cannot,' said Caedmon, 'I do not have sufficient skill to make a poem.' The angel encouraged him: 'Caedmon, sing a song in praise of God the Creator,' and so Caedmon's first poem flowed:

> We worship the Weaver of heaven's wide fabric,
> majesty's Might, the Wisdom of minds,
> creation's Keeper, Maker of marvels,
> glory's Eternity, lordship's Life,
> Who spread out space: for all creatures a canopy;
> Who laid down the land as humanity's home. (Pryce, 2003: 150)

What is it in the angel's commission which releases Caedmon's creativity? Is it the power of relationship which draws forth the poem – sincere encouragement, faith in another's hidden talent as an artist, the angel as appreciative and challenging teacher, mentor, colleague or critic? Perhaps it is also the subjective character of the invitation the angel makes: he invites Caedmon to sing of that which is his everyday experience – the wonderful creation which he inhabits as a herdsman, out with his animals in the fields, woods and hills? Perhaps it is the rooting of Caedmon's personal poetic voice in familiar cultural territory – the communal songs of Scripture and of the Church which he inhabits every day, so that his distinctive and local voice flows out of this universal song, a unique contribution to the vast chorus which is his source and inspiration? Perhaps the angelic inspiration is also theological, calling Caedmon to uncover the divine image which is within him – a freeing of the dynamic human creativity which makes song in response to God the Maker and Creator of all things? Bede's story of Caedmon's calling as a poet grounds his artistic formation in nourishing relationship, authentic experience, generative community, and a dynamic theology of creativity.

In reflecting on my life and work as a Christian and a poet I will trace these themes of divine grace in artistic creativity, while at the same time acknowledging some of the vulnerability and risk which this form of imaginative discipleship entails. The making of poems is an invitation to participate in a divine economy of creativity which characterises what it is to be human, made in the image of the Creator, but this presupposes an artistic faithfulness on my part as a poet. The imaginative flourishing which springs from this faithfulness – which is always gift – depends on trust in fellow poets, artists, audiences and readers, and in the value of my own experience as the stuff from which poems can be made. It draws on the rich resource of the Christian tradition as a source of inspiration and as a focus for my own creation. It is animated by the creative spirit of God at work in my work as a poet. Reflecting on my work within and out of this creative economy, and to explore both the gift which this enterprise gives to me and the response which it demands from me as a poet, I am drawn to Luke's story of the two sons as a narrative about how creative grace is given and enjoyed, but also at risk of being taken for granted and overlooked (Luke 15: 11–32). Pursuing an allegorical interpretation of this story I will explore some of the dynamics of creativity which I experience in the composing of poetry and in sustaining the work and identity of poet (which is always a work in progress), allowing something of the theological character, genius and risk of poetry to emerge along the way. I will explore these questions as a Christian priest, educator, practical theologian and creative writer in the Anglican tradition, drawing on elements of Luke's story to help me unfold my thinking on this dimension of my life and work.

Celebrating the Imaginative Wealth of the Christian Tradition

'Jesus said, "There was a man who had two sons…".'

Jesus tells a story which is about great wealth: a man who is rich in material goods – he has property, a thriving business, servants who work for him and seemingly inexhaustible resources at his disposal. The man is rich also in his relationships and his significance to others. Even as a father this man is rich; he has not one heir, but two: he is a plentiful source of future generations, with every expectation that his progeny will flourish. The story begins with father and sons living in a situation of super-abundance more than sufficient to provide not only for the present, but to cascade down the generations, enriching those who come after. This is a story of patrimony. The father is a source of blessing, a gateway into this great wealth which sustains him and his sons and the household of servants and labourers. It is the story of a bountiful place, a treasury of good things.

If we interpret this immense generative wealth which both father and sons enjoy as being the riches of the imagination, what do the different attitudes and approaches of the characters in the story suggest about the inner dynamics of making poems? My first response is to acknowledge the vast poetic inheritance that I draw on as priest, disciple and pastoral theologian. As a Christian poet I look towards the community of faith as a primary location for source, sustenance and self-understanding. In keeping company with this community, its sacred rituals and texts, and its profound love for language, my imagination has a home in the place where poetry is encountered, nurtured and guarded in an authentic, deep-rooted and nourishing way. Christians are 'people of the book', formed, challenged and sustained by the word of God. Scripture is full of poetry, particularly the Hebrew Scriptures, and in the New Testament some of the most powerful theology takes its shape through song: Mary's 'Magnificat', the self-outpouring God of Philippians, and the victory songs of Revelation depicting heaven as an endless shared performance of uttered praise: all lyrics of utmost beauty, understanding and truth. When Scripture refers to itself, it uses *poetic* language – image and metaphor: 'Your word is a lantern unto my feet and light unto our path' (Psalms 119: 105); 'The word of God … is sharper than any two-edged sword' (Hebrews 4: 12). Poetry is in our DNA as Christians, it constitutes our roots, and it continues to feed us.

This poetry of Scripture nourished Jesus. He quotes the Psalms and the Prophets; the style and content of these references evoke so much more than the few borrowed words say explicitly. He uses poetry to release the theological power of the imagination, as one image gives rise to others, generating a rich harvest of meanings. Jesus' approach to teaching is *poetic*: metaphors, images, stories set alight in the imaginations of his listeners a forest fire of theological insight which can hardly be contained. The craft with which Jesus uses words is more akin to a poet than that of a lawyer or a systematic theologian.

Jesus' followers have come to understand that God's word is more than writing on a page or text in a speech; it is the life of God among us, at work in us and through us. This co-Creator living Word is speaking not only through the Church which hears his voice, but speaks through every human person made in his image, creatively at work in them through the gift of language which distinguishes us from the other animals. Human speaking, writing, reasoning, meaning-making, the whole enterprise of our imagining – this is the power of the original and eternal Word at work in us. Poetry, in its intentional use of language and silence, in the way it plays with meaning and significance, asks us to think about our use of language in constructing our world, witnessing to this living, creative Word. Poetry flows out of an inexhaustible reservoir of creativity within us and between us, a divine dynamic in human artistic form.

Claiming the Poetic Inheritance, Squandering it in Isolation

> '"Father, give me the share of the property that will belong to me".'

The father in this story is very present to both his sons. The younger son speaks directly to him, he listens to what is said, and the father gives generously in response. He invests in his son's potential, and takes the creative risk of handing to the boy what is precious but also vulnerable in unskilled hands. The younger son seems confident: he knows that the family is rich, and he wants to draw immediately on the resources available to him. In asking his father for a share of the wealth the younger son is bold, expectant and adventurous, going off into a distant country under the impression that he is fully funded and adequately equipped. What kind of artistic journey is this that the younger son undertakes? Perhaps a journey deep into the undiscovered places of the self, a foreign country within, full of hidden longings or buried hurts? This is the territory of 'those blue remembered hills ... the land of lost content' in A.E. Housman's imagined Shropshire (1986: 64), and of Sylvia Plath's furious holocaust metaphors in the poem 'Daddy' (Plath, 1965: 54).

Though the younger son may be thought of as adventurous, inquisitive and daring, more conventionally we characterise this curious traveller as reckless, unappreciative and naïve, squandering the father's gift on sources of pleasure that are too expensive for him, searching for meaning in hedonistic delusion. This reckless prodigal son finds himself exhausted and alone, feeding among the pigs. If this story of disaster is also a creative venturing forth, could it represent for us the spending of artistic talent and skill without an appropriate sense of personal discipline, no respect for tradition or expertise? The allegorical meaning here is not to find a moral warning against sexual avarice in the younger son, but to recognise that he is poetry or art trying to inhabit places which are alien and inimitable to creative flourishing, creativity seeking to sustain itself with food which does not nourish. So this may be a particular way of life which kills any possibility of artistic creativity, or an entire culture which stifles freedom of self-expression. So the dancer Nureyev fled the crushing ideological hegemony of Soviet communism, and Auden the propaganda of wartime Britain. When poets like Blake, D.H. Lawrence or Kathleen Raine rail against 'dark satanic mills' of hegemonic mass culture it is not only the creative diminishment of factories and cities that they critique, but also the stifling impact of church and university which cripple the imagination with their own tyrannies of pious moral convention or 'quantitative, scientific "truth"'(Raine, 1975: 16).

The story of the younger son's fruitless self-indulgence and self-obsessiveness, if such a story it is, can also be taken to describe in imaginative terms the risk for creative arts of squandering creativity in chasing emotional thrill, or an illusory impact of public acclaim. It is easy for poetry to find itself starving on the pigswill of inward concerns which are allowed by an undisciplined and isolated talent to produce obscure, self-referential poems which are meaningless outside the poet's particular mind-set. This un-interpretable and uncommunicative 'lyricism', as von Balthasar termed it (Quash, 2007: 23) is one of the great hazards in all artistic endeavour, but particularly in poetry, where the poet can be trapped in an internal monologue of language 'sealed in on itself' (Williams, 2000: xiv). The younger son's isolation and alienation as he thinks back to the wealth of the family home in which even the least in the household enjoy plenty, suggests a longing for relationship and genuine communication with others. In creative terms this longing for fellowship or communion might take the practical form of desperately needing an audience, or of missing a collaborative community of contributors and listeners – *koinonia* as a critical company of fellow poets or responsive readers who appreciate and challenge, colleagues with whom the poet can refine the work to guard against obscurity or self-indulgence. This is Christian community as artistic household, a company of makers and reflectors sharing their produce.

Making the Imaginative Return

'When he came to himself he said, "I will get up and go to my father".'

In the story, at the point of despair the 'prodigal' son takes stock of his situation and returns in his heart and mind to the source of the wealth and security which enabled him to set off in the first place. In this sense he returns to his roots, the place of his origins, and his action in returning I characterise as *poetic* in so far as it seems to me like the conscious engagement in a creative process. The younger brother gathers together the disparate impressions, experiences and half-formed meanings of his shattered life. He does not deny them, but garners them as something precious and brings them 'home' as raw material for the construction of a new life. The younger son carries himself to a place where creativity is possible, to be with the father and the others in the household in some kind of constructive way. That he can hardly have glimpsed what wonders will arise from his desperate, courageous decision to return to source – the welcome of the father, the embrace, the robe, the ring, the feast, the dancing, the attentive servants – what delightful music and rhythm flow from this returning to the place of new-beginning, all this can serve as an illustration of the generous and generative potential of the imagination if it is trusted with the stuff of our lived experience.

The core of the identity of a poet is the activity of making poems, doing the labour of creative construction. This sense of identity is generative – it is in some sense dependent on what the poet produces – though this creativity can be mistaken for something that is to be calculated and monitored, rather than something which is to be appreciated, inhabited and enjoyed. The imaginative pleasure of poetry is found in enjoying the company of the father – keeping closely connected with the imaginative sources within ourselves – and being confident and appreciative in the wealth that is ours because of the father. Being a poet requires resilience, keeping the discipline of paying sustained attention to the world in all its beauty and disfigurement, and to the self in relation to the world, however incomplete and unsatisfactory that may seem to be at any point, and in valuing this experience, however fragmentary or seemingly dysfunctional, for the creative potential that it offers. The younger brother's acknowledgment of his circumstances and experiences in returning to the father is like picking up a pen and capturing the stuff of our life – all its situations, scenes, emotions or encounters – as somehow valuable, somehow food for the imagination, with creative potential for the making of a poem. To be a poet is to be a returner, bringing the random stuff of life to a place where it may be re-configured, and trusting that out of this creative salvage of the imagination will rise new forms which are beautiful, expressive, compelling, true. We have to know the imaginative scrap-value of random experience.

Creativity's Welcome and Embrace

> '"While he was still far off his father saw him and was filled with compassion".'

In the story, the father waits and watches for the lost son. He pays attention hopefully, looking outward from his inward yearning, and with the sharp expectant eye of anticipation he sees the traveller from a great distance, and he goes out to gather up the returner and take him into the home. The watcher embraces even that which is hurtful, alien, not easily or immediately understood. If we interpret the father figure as another dimension of the creative processes of the imagination at work in poetry, then for the watchful eye of the poet nothing is lost in creative ventures, however much energy has been expended, even when the artistic project apparently falters or fails. If the artist returns to the sources of inspiration, then the deep connections will be honoured and renewed. In the same way, the father goes out to the elder brother to embrace his anger and resentment.

In his poem 'Litter stick' the Welsh priest-poet Euros Bowen imagines this artistic enterprise as a kind of *bricolage* – collecting up scraps of images and experiences to be stored in the memory and re-cycled in the imagination as a new creation:

> I saw a man in the garden
> walking the paths and beds
> with a litter stick in his hand,
> picking bits of paper here
> and lifting bits of paper there.
> He looked exactly like a poet
> walking the streets,
> his eyes noticing
> the colour and gesture
> of shops and street-walkers,
> with his stick,
> as though it were acting unawares to himself,
> picking up an image here
> and lifting an image there,
> and quite as unconsciously,
> putting them out of sight
> in the sack on his back.
> His imagination aware,
> so it must have been,
> that he was acting in nature's own way,
> for she too carries colours and gestures
> in her bag,
> and that his litter stick was therefore
> companion to her
> in the task
> of keeping a garden. (Davies and Davies, 1993: 27)

In Bowen's poem about poetry, the poet watches the litter-picker collect his litter and put each item in his sack. As poet he watches attentively, he sees with care, he gathers up the material which attracts him deftly with his sensory stick, and he lodges the image and experience in the unacknowledged sack of his unconscious poetic imagination until he brings it out again as the stuff of a poem – poetic symbols and metaphors – what Coleridge calls 'The lovely shapes and sounds intelligible / Of that eternal language, which thy God / Utters, who from eternity doth teach / Himself in all, and all things in himself' (Guite, 2010: 153). This is the way Nature herself works, says Bowen, a generative dynamic which mirrors the poiesis of God the Word-sending Creator, a creativity in which the poet has a share through the work of the imagination in making art. This is always an act of faith that the artist makes – faith in imagination, both within the self and in collaboration with fellow artists – trusting the welcome that will honour what is brought to the source of creativity for renewal and transfiguration. It takes courage and humility to put pen to paper, to make an artistic act of stepping over the threshold of expression and form; it takes trust that the experience will be one of the imagination rushing forward and being embraced.

The Imagination Longs to Feast and Dance

In the final section of Luke's tale, you will recall that the elder brother returns home from working in the fields, probably exhausted and longing for a bath and his supper. Approaching the farm-house, he hears the extraordinary sound of the music and the dancing, and asks the servants what is going on. 'Your brother has returned' he is told, 'and your father is celebrating because he has him back safe and sound.' The dutiful son is furious; he refuses to enter the house and join in the celebration. The father comes out to him and pleads with him to join the party. But the elder son is so hurt and offended by the favour being shown to his reckless brother that he cannot overcome his anger: 'For years I have served you like a slave without question, yet for me there has never been even the smallest celebration.' The father is astonished that this obedient, flawless child of his has so little understanding of the resources which have been at his disposal, and such fragile confidence in the love and deep regard in which he is held: 'Son, you are always with me, and all that is mine is yours.' This virtuous and industrious man is able to do the work of a son, but not to enjoy the love in which he is held as a child of his father. Standing alone on the margins, the elder son hardly knows who he is, nor how lovingly he is regarded. He has built his identity as son on dutiful labour; he has yet to become in his own heart and mind the son that he is in the eyes of the father.

For me, becoming part of the Diviners, joining a company of poets, has helped me to understand myself as a poet in a new way, and to accept the description of 'poet' as something which holds true to my identity. This is the first writing group I have been part of, and the first time I have shared my writing with other writers who make an explicit link between the art of poetry and the practice of faith. It is a bit like joining the party, coming into the house from an isolated enterprise to share in a celebration! Being a poet is a matter of practice, of course – writing poems is something I have done since childhood, and some have been published, in school magazines and other publications. But reading poems to other poets as part of the Diviners group, having to find some material to share at each meeting, receiving appreciation and critical feedback, responding to the poetry of others in the group, and being invited to reflect on my poetry in a theological way – all this is for me a formational process by way of becoming a poet. In fact, this is the first time since childhood I have looked back over my life and attempted to gather together poems I have written in a way which enables me to say something about what that work has been and is about.

I'm reminded of how the prologue to Benedict's *Rule* speaks of the monastery as 'a school for the Lord's service' (Barry, 1997: 4). Benedict offers individuals a creative discipline of living, working and praying with other disciples in community in a way which makes the spiritual commitment of discipleship apparent, intentional and accountable. Living in community enables the aspiring disciple to become a follower of Christ in a way which is more deeply held and sustained; it gives a way of Christian faith to become a shared enterprise, a practice to be enjoyed with others. Diviners is a similar experience for me: it makes a space for the work of the imagination, the making of poems – the poiesis – to be acknowledged, owned, refined, developed. The shared enterprise between poets enables me to keep on becoming a poet, perhaps as the worship and fellowship of church enables me to keep on becoming a believer, and the mutual support and accountability of the collegiality of priests to keep on becoming a priest, and the love, demand and challenge of relationships to keep on becoming a person.

Poetry and the Spiritual Pleasure of Being a Christian

'" Son, you are always with me, and everything I have is yours".'

In this story it seems that the more virtuous of the two sons is the elder brother, who is dutiful and loyal and keeps close to his father. Yet he lacks the capacity to appreciate or enjoy the extraordinary inheritance that is his patrimony. This elder brother lives on the estate and maintains it, but he cannot take pleasure in the good things in which he has been welcome to participate, so that the father's generosity to his wayward sibling wounds and enrages him. He is scrupulous to a fault, and in artistic terms this very conventionality may have stifled him, holding him back from experimentation with form or inhibiting him from including dimensions of his experience in his creative work. So Auden encouraged his composer friend Benjamin Britten to relinquish the conventional, adoring environments which he created for himself and to engage with 'the demands of disorder', the wilder hedonistic dimensions of himself, so as to mature in his art (Kildea, 2013: 197). The dutiful son holds back from engaging in the pleasure of company which he regards as unmerited. So many faithful Christians recognise ourselves in this narrative – maintaining the family business of the church and sustaining the religious economy through thick and thin – but to a degree which can deaden us to the spiritual beauty and spontaneity of the faith. Like the busy, hard-working brother (a cousin to busy, hard-working Martha?) we lose the capacity for contemplation, for play, and forget the sometimes reckless and undeserved generosity of God's grace. Poetry can call us back into the company of the Creator, and open us up to appreciate the beauty and giftedness of people and approaches different from ourselves, slowing us down, arresting us so that we look and listen to our inner world and the world without.

A dimension of this resistance to gracious company and spiritual pleasure is that too often the cautious church forgets her poets, refusing to go in to the party where language, experience and imagination make merry. Though a tendency in Christianity, and particularly in Protestantism, is towards logo-centrism, for all our preaching and prose-writing, do we demonstrate much care or artistry with words? How many Christians enjoy the wealth of poetry that is our inheritance, and the respect for the value of words which poetry demands? Poetry certainly does not have a monopoly on the imagination, nor is it everyone's preference, but the patterns and meanings of words and silences in poetry are fundamental to what we deal with as ministers and disciples – the words of Scripture, of liturgy and prayer, the words of comfort, eulogy, proclamation, teaching, celebration and lament. Words play in poems; they may assume different characteristics: they are ambivalent, they are multivalent, they are simple, complex, insightful, profound, perplexing or confusing. As Christians we need to be artful, considerate and considered dealers in words. Where words are treasured as creative sources of energy and healing, poems tend to well up in witness to healing and transformation, like springs at the ancient sites of martyrdom. My experience is that the Diviners are one community in which this creative wealth is counted out and appreciated, and using poetry in Quiet Days, retreats and sermons I encounter many other individuals and groups who recognise the power of poetry to bring alive the spiritual pleasure of faith as a source of healing, strength and sheer existential delight.

The Prophetic and Liberative Imperative of Poetry

> '"…we have to celebrate – this brother of yours was dead and has come to life,
> he was lost and has been found".'

The elder brother has grown comfortable with his accustomed dialogue between father and son; he had not known that there were voices missing, nor is he keen to hear an unfamiliar story. The father wants to hear the story of the son and to celebrate its telling; he wants to raise up the fallen child with dignity and honour the one who shares his brokenness and sin: the imagination will not exclude what may count as marginal, nor can it overlook injustice. The imagination is prophetic (Brueggemann, 1983, 1989) in its call for integrity and lived moral courage, and the language of the prophets is poetry, which interrogates, inspires, convicts and inflames the hearts of the faithful. Pastoral and Practical Theologians have emphasised this capacity of poetry to foster critical reflection on experience in a manner which grasps the shape and significance of events in ways which are expansive rather than reductionist. A poem can attend to the particular and specific, even to the momentary, distilling meaning in ways which are profoundly faithful to the given-ness of the event but open up new possibilities, different interpretations, attending to and re-framing experience (Capps, 1993).

The power of language is fundamental in re-fashioning human identity and experience, and poetry focuses this, drawing attention to the connections or fractures between experience, idealogies, words and meanings. Poetical language seeks to animate the imagination and to stir the heart through use of language as a life-enhancing, transformational resource in new ideas and understandings (Alves, 1990; Pattison and Woodward, 1994; Pattison, 2000). Practical Theology even describes its approach as 'poetical' in its hermeneutical, transformational task, telling and re-telling narratives, making and re-making the socially constructed world of our theory and practice (Veling, 2005). In poetry, excluded individuals and groups have a seat at the table and find a voice which is powerful because it is authentic, speaking out of experience and context in ways which do justice to complex situations through its capacity for nuanced multivalency. Indeed, Ellen Davis suggests that such a large proportion of the words of the Hebrew Scriptures are in poetic form because poetry is the language 'best suited to probing the inexhaustible mystery of the human situation in its *entirety* … poetry looks at phenomena whole' (Davis, 2000: 19).

The Creative Patrimony of a Christian Poet

In exploring the identity of being a poet and a Christian through Luke's story of the father and the two sons I have characterised that identity as a creative enterprise which draws on inexhaustible reserves. These are the dynamic resources of the creative imagination which yield works of beauty, wisdom and insight from the great range of human experiences shaped into poems. Where in this story is the wife and mother, the mistress of the estate? Where are the sisters, her daughters? What story would they tell? This absence has fascinated many theologians and artists, and is a lacuna which seems to generate its own art (Slee and Cameron, forthcoming). In Chapter 15 the preceding story is of a wealthy woman who has 10 coins. In contrast to the rich father and his sons, this woman knows the value of what she has, and when she loses even a small part of it, a single coin, she sweeps her house and searches thoroughly until she finds it again, and rejoices with her friends and neighbours when she rediscovers what is hers (Luke 15: 8–10). She counts the treasure – not in a miserly way – but in an appreciative way that seems lacking in the approach of the father and his sons. This is the approach of feminine Wisdom who rejoices in the works of creation, and plays in the presence of God like a child (Proverbs 8: 22ff) – that is, like one whose creative imagination is neither shackled nor squandered, and for whom the making of art is an activity of value for its own sake (Hugo Rahner, 1965; Davis, 2000: 66–9).

So let me count the treasure. As an Anglican I become more and more conscious of the wealth of Christian poetry and art which I have available to me through the tradition in which I have been formed and on which I continue to draw as a pastor and poet. The creative capital which funds imaginative life is not only the wealth of individual talent, but also an inheritance which is corporate, both cultural and ecclesial: the accumulation of the poetry of many people, places and phases of history to which the imagination has given rise, and which enables the individual to flourish and participate. The Church of England's calendar includes holy men and women who are remembered particularly for their poetry: Richard Rolle, George Herbert, John Donne, Thomas Traherne, John Keble, Christina Rossetti, Evelyn Underhill, Geoffrey Studdert-Kennedy (Tristam, 1997; Atwell, 1998; Church of England, 2000). Anglicanism has its roots in English poetry (Rowell et al., 2001: 8–9), and this inheritance is dynamic, continuing to foster new creation inspired by writers whom Stephen Spender, in his eulogy for T.S. Eliot, calls 'the more living / the dead' (Spender, 1994: 46). Some write out of experience as pastors and priests – David Scott (1984, 1989), Rowan Williams (2001, 2008), Manon Ceridwen (2013), Rachel Mann (2013); other poets explore the experience, character and language of Christian faith in contemporary culture – Geoffrey Hill (1985, 1996, 2002), Micheal O'Siadhail (1999), Michael Symmons Roberts (2004, 2013), Mary Oliver (2007, 2008), Roger McGough (2012). Some are distanced from the faith or have no professed faith at all, yet do a kind of religious work in helping us to celebrate and refine our sense of the world as a place of wonder and tragedy in language which cannot fail to compel, challenge and inspire. Of these, whom shall I say? Carol Ann Duffy is pre-eminent, perhaps. This is a living craft, and it witnesses to the gift of life in and through the gift of language. To this continuing gift we should attend as Christians, with joy and thanksgiving. In his essay 'Poetry and the Christian' Karl Rahner commends all poetry, both explicitly religious and 'secular', as profoundly and spiritually valuable because poetry addresses the deepest levels of the human heart and so prepares us for the eternal word of the gospel: 'there is a brightness and a secret promise in every word ... the capacity and the practice of perceiving the poetic word is a presupposition of hearing the word of God' (Karl Rahner, 1982: 362–3). Poetry need not talk about God or be composed by those who believe in God to prepare the human heart to receive the divine truth and light of God in Christ.

My introduction to this poetic wealth was through the choral tradition. Singing and saying the words and songs of the liturgy four or five times a week for all my childhood years steeped me in the cadences, rhythms, metaphors of the psalms and canticles and hymns. The poetical dimension of Jesus' teaching, his images and stories, and the wonderful rhetoric of prophets and apostles, I found compelling: magical language invoking in me a love of beauty, a world beyond the mundane market town reality. The church was and continues to be a major source of literary and artistic formation for me, a place where words are to be pondered over as multi-faceted dynamic creatures, with their roots deep down in other cultures and languages. Yet the local church can also constrain horizons. Growing up in Oswestry, Wilfred Owen's birth-place, in the 1960s and 70s when the memory of world war was still vivid in the minds of the many men who had served in the forces, I cannot recall encountering Owen's poetry, nor hearing his name mentioned in church or even in school. Perhaps his work was too challenging for war veterans, or too difficult, or simply not sufficiently well-known? Although formal education in 1960s Shropshire was not the most inspiring, teachers encouraged 'creative writing' as a way of developing language skills – even for boys! Words were to be celebrated, experiences explored and feelings taken for a ride in free-style poetry, and alongside the liturgical world of Bible and Prayer Book as a well-stocked larder of metaphor and a rich collection of form and style, creative writing gave me access to the power of poetic language as a form of self-expression and public representation.

When, at 16, I began to 'question my faith', it was the poetry of R.S. Thomas (which I discovered quite by accident in the one book shop in town) that seemed to offer 'doubt' not as a lapse in belief but as an imaginative project, even a priestly vocation, if this religious struggle could somehow be explored and expressed with apt beauty. For example, R.S. Thomas's poem 'The New Mariner' (Thomas, 1993: 338), reworking Coleridge's 'Ancient Mariner' metaphor of voyage as religious journey, introduced to me in exquisitely lucid and sensitive language the ancient possibilities of apophatic spirituality as a way of creatively addressing the difficulties of faith in the scientific, rational age. This is a continuation of the honest spiritual wrestling of the poetry of The Psalms, of Job, of the Suffering Servant who sings his songs of lament (Isaiah 52:13–53:12). My experience of the time was that, more than sermons or other forms of public theological interpretation and spiritual guidance, poetry embraced the difficult, hidden experience of religious doubt, gave expression to it, and offered an analysis which was descriptive, evocative, accurate yet nuanced, a way of interpreting experience in ways which apprehended meaning and accessed wisdom without reducing them to glib summaries.

On one level poetry sets a tone for the practice of religion, fosters an ethos: to be a believer is to encounter doubt; faithfulness is the practice of engaging with the whole range of religious experience and with the mysteries of encounter with the Divine, the God who hides his face as well as reveals himself. Poetry becomes a kind of travel writing for the religious journey, tracing the different landscapes, climates, cultures. But it is more than an inventory or report. In addressing the different dimensions of religious experience with the kind of serious engagement that poetry allows, engaging memory both corporate and personal, animating the imagination, poetry becomes the language for exploring life as lived, a place where questioning or speculation can be entertained, new perspectives opened-up, the particularities of experience, situation, context celebrated, lamented, analysed, integrated, ambivalences or contradictions somehow held in tension.

Attending to my Work as a Poet in the Christian Poetic Tradition

The poems which I have included in the section which follows give a flavour of my work to date and the interests which have inspired me as a writer and which I seek to address in my writing. Some of the work is intensely personal, like 'Lazarus Blossom', written as an elegy for Bishop Peter Walker, which reflects on experiencing the hope of resurrection as a salvaging of valuable experiences and memories in the transitory present – a practice which poetry can help us to do. Poetry gathers yet also transforms experience. The poem 'Girl playing with a magic cloth' is a domestic and familial poem in so far as it arose from the memories of one delightful afternoon when I was playing with my nieces in the garden; the imaginative capacity of a child to create worlds through her games became my way of celebrating the creative, inexhaustibly generative power of the imagination which I felt moved to celebrate particularly on the occasion of the appointment of Carol Ann Duffy as the first woman Poet Laureate. Duffy's influence is apparent in the next poem 'Contours Shop Window, Selly Oak' which celebrates the shy beauty of a window display in a local ladies' outfitters, and in particular the sounds of the brands of the different merchandise, each of which was lovingly written by hand on pink cards laid over each item. This is the poetry of ordinary language, poetry as a form of ethnography, exploring the local culture. It is the poetry of a parish priest walking her patch, coming to know its sights and sounds intimately, making an interpretation of place, loving parochial eccentricities.

The poem 'Bring rest sweet dreaming child' was written as a personal meditation on the Incarnation which I decided to share in the sermon at Midnight Mass when a parish priest in Smethwick. Subsequently it was set to music by the composer Tarik O'Regan for a commission to be performed in a Carol Service at St Paul's Covent Garden, and so I added the designation 'Carol' to the title. It is an example of how as a poet I have worked with musicians and other artists in creative projects, and the opportunity for this kind of creative collaboration is one of the joys of being a poet associated with worshipping communities and the music and art which they sustain. In this way the poetry of personal reflection becomes a kind of public theology.

The poem 'How to live under occupation' is on the one hand an historical reflection on what it might have been like for citizens to live with integrity when their country has been invaded by a conquering army, but it is also a poem about the ideological politics of any community in which identity and power are an issue, and also a personal reflection on what it means to live as an individual with the inner occupying forces of hurt, grief or emotional pain following loss or assault. The poem which follows, 'A New Commandment', is also a poem about living with conflict, written at the close of a Bridge Builders *Transforming Conflict* course at Whirlow Grange, Sheffield in 2012, just as spring exploded in the garden and woods around the house. It is a personal reflection on Scripture, and also a way of reflecting theologically on the impact of the training, as well as a poem which critically examines the potentially evasive tendency of some poetry influenced by Romantic ideals, focusing on the search for the divine in

Nature rather than in the challenges of fallen human relationships which need redemption.

Masculinities, Gender and Practical Theology

The poems which follow were first published in *Finding a Voice* (Pryce, 1996) which offered a theological analysis of Men's Studies and the critical examination of masculinity as it had developed in the 1980s and 1990s in response to feminism and the women's movement, as well as other liberation movements. The poems show the influence of theologians who were inviting men to re-imagine their sexuality and identity in the light of feminism and gay liberation (Nelson, 1992; Culbertson, 1994), and the poems were one way in which I undertook explorations into the identity and performance of masculinity which integrated theology, gender studies and personal experience – or at least, held them together in dialogue without forcing a conclusion, playing with non-patriarchal models of masculinity as I reflect on Scripture and tradition. 'Born of a Woman' reflects on Renaissance images of the adoration of the Christ Child presented by his mother to the magi as a naked human being: in the kenosis and sacrificial servant ministry of Jesus the phallocentric and patriarchal ideologies of religion are surpassed. 'Minister's Song' suggests that men in ministry have a vulnerability with which they can connect, share with other men in ministry and find a new brotherhood free from clerical competitiveness and disguised fear. 'The Burial' explores the idea of how the radical nature of Christian discipleship re-genders spiritual identity and practice through the motif of Joseph of Arimathea preparing the wounded body of Jesus for burial: this wealthy, powerful and seemingly invulnerable man is doing messy 'feminine' work – a midwife after the salvic birth of the cross.

Poetry as the Continuing Unfolding of the Scriptures and a Companion to Liturgy

One of my contributions is to promote poetry as a resource for the spirituality and worshipping life of Christian communities and individuals. I have compiled and edited two *Literary Companions for Sundays* (Pryce, 2001) and for *Festivals* (Pryce, 2003) to offer poems drawn from the great tradition of Christian poetry, women as well as men, and from diverse times and cultures, and in addition to Caedmon's *Hymn* (see the beginning of this chapter) I include another translation of an ancient poem as an example of how the contemporary poet can bring his art to interpret and re-present the poetic tradition of the church for contemporary believers. 'Bede's Death Song' (Pryce, 2003: 55) reminds us that integral to the Venerable Bede's scholarship was a skill in poetry – among his many learned works is *De Arte Metrica*, a treatise on the craft and discipline of composing verse. This verse was said by one of Bede's pupils to have been uttered by him in vernacular English as he drew close to death. The poem 'Joachim and Anne read *Proverbs*' (Pryce, 2003: 90–91) imagines the parents of the Blessed Virgin Mary looking back on the scandalous pregnancy of their daughter, contemplating its outrageousness and its mystery. The reference to Proverbs is to chapter 31, which extols the gifts of moral goodness in women – a vision of feminine spiritual virtue which is at once transgressed, fulfilled and superseded by Mary's mysterious childbearing.

This imaginary approach to reflection on Scripture is represented in the remainder of the poems, all of which arose out of conversations about the gospels with practical theologian James Woodward and biblical scholar Paula Gooder, whose theological insight, and that of our commissioning editor at SPCK, Ruth McCurry, encouraged me to pursue poetry as a valid, powerful and generative form of unfolding the scriptures. My partnership with them is an example of how poetry can grow out of co-operation across theological disciplines and bear fruit in the interpretative and evangelistic work of the churches.

'Jesus is baptised in the River Jordan' from *Journeying with Mark* (Woodward, Gooder and Pryce, 2011) imagines what the river itself might say following the baptism – the idea of one natural phenomenon speaking on behalf of all creation about the cosmic significance of the Saviour. Also included are some sections from 'Lenten Bestiary' in which 'the wild beasts' of Mark's temptation wilderness (Mark 1: 1–15) are ascribed a character or role, becoming psychological beasts as well as living creatures to indicate the human vulnerability of Jesus, simultaneously subject to the physical forces of nature and the inner struggles of isolation, displacement and doubt. Some wild beasts are threatening, some delightful: they gather around Jesus as the new Adam, the one come to restore creation to its original God-intended harmony (Genesis 1: 1–2: 4). The ministering angels are interpreted here as personifications of consolation, messengers of divine presence, guidance and support in times of trouble and spiritual agony.

Across the five sections they have the character of the five senses: sight, taste, hearing, smell, touch. This way of working suggests how the imaginative scope of poetry enables the development of a slender theological theme evoked in the Scriptural text, in a way which fosters deeper theological understanding and spiritual sustenance for the journey of faith. I can trace the influence of Thomas Merton's work in this poetic sequence (Merton, 1977).

Choosing poems from *Journeying with Luke* (Woodward, Gooder and Pryce, 2012), 'The sense of him' stays with the five physical senses as a meditation on what it is to encounter the man Jesus, whose physicality and theological identity seem so interwoven in the gospels. This poem, and others from the Luke volume, were set to music under the direction of Richard Pinel and sung during the Holy Week liturgies at St George's Chapel Windsor in 2013. Luke's second volume, Acts of the Apostles, is full of references to the inspiration of the Holy Spirit in the lives of early Christians; 'The Holy Spirit talks to fellow witnesses...' unfolds an imaginary pneumatology constructed from these narratives as the Spirit (entirely out of character!) speaks about himself rather than in and through the lives of others. The third poem 'The story continues ...' celebrates Luke's story-telling Jesus and the power of story to unleash a generative creative dynamic for individuals and communities as they inhabit story for themselves and pass on the tale in new ways – a narrative gospel rippling out to others.

Finally, *Journeying with Matthew* (Woodward, Gooder and Pryce, 2013) takes up the particular emphasis in the early chapters of Matthew's gospel, which foreground Joseph's part in the story of salvation. 'The house that Joseph built' honours Joseph's skill as a carpenter, and also the perseverance and patience he displays as a spiritual craftsman in extraordinary circumstances as the husband of Mary and guardian of Jesus. Here the ballad form seems to allow the strange challenge and blessing of God's healing work to emerge, as it does with such effect in the poems of Charles Causley (1997). The final poem 'Patterns in words' takes Matthew's 'compositional habit' of presenting his gospel material in triads, and focusing on Matthew's passion narrative traces this threefold structure to give emphasis to the theological themes of Jesus' betrayal, trial, execution and burial.

Lazarus Blossom

Turning out the vase of wilted roses
I find three buds, expectant
Still white, still fragrant
As if still opening.

In keeping these last flowers
(crystal cleaned, fresh water)
I declare them to be also
Blooms from the first flush, the ever-new.

May this harvest be a regular blessing:
To pluck out of each fading
More than reprieve, more than salvage,
Even the gleanings of a resurrection.

Girl playing with a magic cloth

She spreads a cloth across the lawn.
Walk there she says
Underneath is a tunnel
Which goes into the deepest cavern of the earth.

She spreads a cloth upon the lawn.
Sit here she says
Now we are on an island
With tigers, lizards and coconuts.

She spreads a cloth out on the grass
Lie here she says
This is a bed
on which your mother made a baby brother.

She spreads a cloth upon the grass.
Sleep here she says
This is the chair
in which your Daddy snores.

She spreads a cloth into the grass.
Jump! Jump! she says.
This is a hole dug out of the ground
This is the grave they put your Granny in she says.

'Contours' Shop Window, Selly Oak

Like an older woman in the queue,
on this Parade too easily overlooked,
positioned as you are behind the bus-stop,
demure between the Butchers' blare of
blood red, fluorescent orange special offers
and Manyana Sauna's neon lure
bubbling day and night above unyielding mirror-glass and blanked-out doors
whose signs say 'Entrance at the rear'.

Your business is entirely apparent, and
you have your own allure
for retired headmistresses, for Barbara Pym,
Miss Marple and any sensible, independent-minded lady
who will understand the quiet confidence of a sitting tenant,
your art of being discreetly present
from one rare purchase to another.

For complete appreciation of your beauty
one must come at it obliquely, and with special care,
as if not to startle birds, or children at play.
Peering into your frontage
requires the delicacy of dusting ornaments,
moving a flower arrangement,
undressing a corpse.
You are all display,
An unmistakable intention of availability –
Almost any item which a customer might need,
But no compulsion, just offering.
Your deft hand-written cards
Set down so gently on to pastel colours
Or propped against the softness and the durability of reputable fabrics,
Look how they finger their suggestions into
Folds of skin and purse
As comfort and economy make exquisite love
Of a hesitant kind
in the sales-talk of your labelling.

And each with its own careful price:
Twilfit, Excelsior, Court Royal, Faun,
Berlei, Naturana, Exquisite Form,
Playtex, Gossaro, Vedonis, White Swan,
Contours, Nymphit, Aristoc, Pierre Balmain;
A side-hook girdle, a summer skirt, a mock quilt house-coat, pretty short-sleeved tops
A fleecy bed jacket, a smooth cup, lined skirts, and lovely jumpers,
Faun roll-ons, cotton comfort, bed socks in assorted colours.

CAROL: Bring rest sweet dreaming child[1]

If you came at night,
Pushing your way down the long dark
Out into starlight;
Come now into our anxious, sleepless hours:
Bring rest, sweet dreaming child.

If you came at dawn,
Lifting a voice from the dumb void,
Your new song born;
Speak now into our shouting, stifled days:
Bring praise, sweet singing child.

If you came at day's
Noon, spreading out your arms to shade
From anger's fierce sun-blaze;
Reach now into our frenzied, drifting years:
Bring peace, sweet trusting child.

If you came at dusk,
Warming our chill fears with the blood
Of love's sure pulse;
Touch now the numb limbs of our fading lives:
Bring love, sweet breathing child.

---

[1] Originally published as the text for a composition by Tarik O'Regan (2004).

How to live under occupation

It was like waking up to strange news
From a radio that had played all night
Through sleep:
The drone became language, meaning,
Then pain.

Land we had believed to be ours,
Land that was ours, is still –
Places we imagined ourselves free,
The uncomplicated valleys,
Sun-warmed woods of wild garlic and cherry blossom,
A terroir beautifully sounded with the song-flit of bird –
Beyond these, beneath them,
As if from deep earth
A hellish rumble of tanks and the ruptured gear changes of troop-carriers:
An alien melody of invasion.

Living now
In what we have come to understand as occupied territory
We must decide whose is the domain,
And what then might living be.
In the safe jurisdiction of lock and key
Each paper deed of property is filed away in order;
Their grammar can define the particularities of ownership
In feet and inches, boundaries and values
And with exquisite accuracy
Taught us to recite the rhetoric of voluntary exchange.

But now there is an energy which does not speak,
So vital it precedes restraints of word or letter.
The meres are soured, our verges mined,
And it will kill with absolute disregard.
Events have handed us a summons,
A kind of requisition,
And we must now decide in what manner we shall abide here,
Whether to submit, or to resist, or both, and how.

Each day for us becomes a question to inhabit, a predicament,
Performance not dissimilar to the trauma of love, or of hate:
'Whose is the body which seethes so?'
Are we the possession of our lovers, of our enemies, our memories, our sicknesses?
Having made the diagnosis
Then the issue becomes
How to live under occupation.

A New Commandment

John 13:34 – Love moving towards conflict

Poets have a tendency
towards daffodils,
trees,
the lifting up of eyes towards hills.

This was your convention too:
'Look at the birds... the flowers... how a branch puts forth its buds...'

But you turn our gaze also
towards the less appealing:
the festering argument,
the dirty feet,
to your own strange wounds;

inviting us to find in these
God's beauty, our beauty.

Born of a woman²

Matthew 2:11

Beneath the mound of his belly
In the valley of his thighs
At source,
Is the tuber
With the two tiny bulbs
Which root and swell in Nazareth, Galilee, Gethsemane's garden
Stiffening up into the lush tree of Calvary's cross.

Minister's Song³

Luke 18: 35–43

Do not mistake me for the strong one.
The poor man in me
Reaches to the poor man
In you:
Crying child comforting
Crying child.
Together, unseen
We will sit by the side of the road
And watch the fast parts of us
Speeding by
In their smooth, impenetrable cars.

---

² Originally published in Pryce (1996: 146).
³ Ibid.

The Burial[4]

John 19: 39

On the edge of the evening I make your bed
Deep in a place without light,
Heaving up the slumpen haul of you
To wrap the sheets and resin round
As if to give you shelter from the wind.

No wind in this stone womb,
Only the winding,
The probe of massage
At your breathless form;
My ancient, learned, insufficient ointment spreads
In tests across your flesh to
Pool around the obscene wounds.
Are they the blush of love
Or shame?

This is my second undertaking in the dark:
I found you once before at night,
Heavy then with questions, coming down
The long dim uterine folds of hidden search
From which you tugged me
Into blinding light.
Having seen
Your thrash upon the wood,
Your pain that chased away the sun,
The push and cry and surge and pang
I grope again around the obscure breaking out
Of something new,
Anticipating birth.

Yet not a breath of wind
Nor movement but my own,
Death's midwife – here
To cut the binding cord and tie a knot,
All wonder at your seeping holes.
How can it be that these are openings
To let new traffic in the Spirit
Come and go?

---

[4]   Originally published in Pryce (1996: 150).

Joachim and Anne read *Proverbs*[5]

It was not what we had come to expect of her –
not after the years of tuition,
household economics and steady religion,
the careful selection of a decent husband;
not after all our efforts to ensure
that she should be wise and well provided for
out of her own resourcefulness,
an excellent woman –

The sudden (hidden) stain of her child
before time,
the fearful seeping out of shame,
the tearing of code and convention,
unravelling us.

She surprised:
to her the boy came
like an unfolding of exquisite cloth for a wedding,
stuff more precious than ever we could have bought,
more intricate than we could have made with all our care,
she had woven within her.
And (thank God) the husband proved better
than even we had calculated:
he seemed to see her clothed in that same dress,
a garment utterly beyond us,
gracious, compelling, powerfully modest –
as if our daughter had gained access
to some heavenly loom.

---

[5]   Originally published in Pryce (2003: 90–91).

Bede's *Death Song* (a translation)[6]

No one is wiser than he need be,
Considering that certain journey which every one must make,
To take account, before the soul sets out,
What good there is, and evil,
With which the spirit may be judged
After his death day.

---

[6]   Originally published in Pryce (2003: 55).

Jesus is baptised in the River Jordan[7]

Mark 1: 4–11

When he stepped into me, it was then I became pure.

Though I had washed a million stinking garments,
carrying away in my flow
rain after rain
the stain of your industry and ablution,
your bleaching and dyeing and tanning –
not to mention the defecation of cities and sheep;

Though I have rinsed the skin of lepers clean,
flushed disease
and the blood of your wars
downstream,
out through my veins
with the elemental force that was mine since The Flood;

Though I perform all these miracles of cleansing for you,
you children of Eve and Adam,
dreamers of clear streams in the well-watered garden,
children of Moses, who turned Egyptian rivers to run with blood
and conjured seas to step aside for your escape;
though you hanker after purity and freedom
all your pollutions I have had to hold…

It was not until his calloused feet were planted on my smoothed-stone bed,
when I made my cold embrace of his calves (a walker's legs he had),
and played my swift dart in and out of the thighs
to see if I could topple him –
it was not until John swelled him down into me
with the long pour and the plunge…

only then I flowed freely
free as I did when the dove first drew me
out of deep dark chaos,
and now every sweet drop of me
standing in stone jars and welling up in fonts
tastes of the finest wine

newly infused as I am
with the life-force
for which all living things have waited.

---

[7]   Originally published in Woodward, Gooder and Pryce (2011: 48–9).

Sections from **A Lenten Bestiary in the company of angels**[8]

Mark 1:13

The first wild beast, first angel

The wild dove sings to comfort a solitary figure:

Not all is alien here in the desert.
Yes, there are the harsher birds with their appetite for dead things,
Keeping open a constant eye for carrion or prey.
But there are those of us, hiding in the clefts of the rocks, who sing,
Keeping one another company year after year.
Remember it was one such as I
Who found the evidence for an end to animosity,
Flying over miles of watery waste
To gladden Noah's heart
As I will gladden yours
If only you will listen, morning and evening
To my quiet song
As it puts forth gently, like an olive branch,
Sound of the whole cosmos sounding out in praise.

The sight of the rainbow angel of the Covenant painting the sky:

Displaying my stock of ochres and azures
I daub down the steep bank of sky
Colouring the bond between earth and heaven
Which the Maker of all things has set for a sign.

Look, look, I cry to those who are hurting,
To those who are bitter, or worn-down, or sad;
See what delight the Lord has for his creatures,
Look to the rainbow to know how things are.

The third wild beasts, third angel

The angry black dogs of depression and disillusionment:

The last thing we expected
Was for you to befriend us.
We tracked you for days at a distance,
Lurking behind,
Threatening, growling,
Needing you to fear us,
To deny to yourself that we were there.

---

[8] Originally published in Woodward, Gooder and Pryce (2011: 58–64).

But you called us down, you named us, stroked us like children,
Let us lie around you, calm.
With you there is no pretence, not even to self.
And the anger which fuels us,
This you acknowledge
And send bounding out to fetch back sticks for you,
Turned into play.

The angel of sacrifice imparts the loving art of smell:

Not the stench of cattle, sheep and doves
That he longs for now,
But the smell of the beloved,
Grasped firm, pulled close and held for ever,
That unmistakable scent
Of skin, the breath, the hair...
This is what he treasures.

The fifth wild beast, fifth angel

Elephants, wolves, lions, flies:

We see the human figure sitting hunched, alone.
We desire that you become the prey of envy, of isolation,
That you should long to hunt and hurt as we do:
For we are beasts of herd, of pack, of pride, of swarm,
We trample and devour;
We defend ourselves, we dominate each other,
We never deviate.
To us the loner is vulnerable, ailing,
And we shall tear him limb from limb
As he hates himself for having no one to lie next to him.

The touch of the angel who comforts the lonely:

I am the angel of Solitude,
And I hold its precious ointment in my gentle hands.
My service is to soothe the inner ache of loneliness.
My balm will ease you,
Free you from the emptiness which grips you like a pain.
My fingers shall unleash you
To play in the astonishing presence of God,
I shall unbind you
To welcome the beauty of your own true self.

The sense of him[9]

The sight of him would be
gentle light of a child's face,
bright flame in cold dark
warming us.

The sound of him would be
steady beat of the sleeper's breath,
calm voice in a wild storm
taming it.

The smell of him would be
unwashed, acrid, from the road,
fish off his friends' boats
repelling us.

The touch of him would be
rasp of worker's calloused hands
graze of rough cloth, damp,
becoming glorious.

The taste of him would be
sweet yeast of shared bread, torn, passed:
desert food, salt tears
filling us.

---

[9]   Originally published in Woodward, Gooder and Pryce (2012: 41).

The Holy Spirit talks to fellow witnesses…[10]

We are witnesses to these things, and so is the Holy Spirit whom God has given to those who obey him (Acts 5:32)

It may seem to you as if I do not have a voice.
How does fire speak? How does light?
Must love have words?
Not always.

Sometimes I am sheer energy, sometimes touch, sometimes stillness;
Mostly you can trace me in the quality of experience,
As a body senses out the way it dreams of being through a dance;
I am at play when a child leaps in the womb.
To know me is like the seeping-in of morning,
A shift from one world to another,
The power of becoming.

I move through walls, through the cells of flesh and prisons;
I open hearts and minds and eyes and ears and doors of every kind.
Being the Giver of gifts, I surprise –
You become my voice through a language not your own, which strangers understand,
With a song you sing in chains I may enchant the desolate.
I lead you in the finding-out of unfamiliar places:
Journey after journey becomes your home with me,
For I am a way of travelling,
I am your disturber, your companion, the interpreter
Of visions and of blinding moments.
Both the flow and the fracture may be evidence for my involvement.
I may overwhelm, I may conceal myself;
Listen for me, look for me, wait patiently with the patience I shall give
Until a time of my choosing.

---

[10]   Originally published in Woodward, Gooder and Pryce (2012: 73–4).

The story continues... [11]

Most of what remains beyond the telling
he leaves to you, if you have ears to hear.
The art of story is to unlock doors, pull back shutters, open up perspectives,
to create a world from nothing and leave its future in your hands.
You are free to tie down his words as solutions,
but what he has unleashed in you
is possibilities.
For the story is free as the heart's freedom.
Each one is a garden which he leases
for just the peppercorn rent of your soul's attention.
Then: all yours!

What will you do with this gift of space?
Play in it?
Trace its boundaries?
Find its hidden places?
Run wild there like a child to discover your many selves?
Till it and tend it through seasons for the strange fruits it will bear?

Listener, reader, imaginer,
Do anything with what is yours, if you have heart and mind and soul and strength,
do anything except wall it up and keep trespassers out.
If it's rules you like,
then for God's sake make up a game and pretend to be a trespasser yourself,
so you can see how it feels to be in the wrong,
to be chased out, or welcomed in with the surging grace of forgiveness.
For the story is a live thing, to be nurtured;
it is a crafted thing to be worn;
it is a fund to be traded.
To enter a story is to set out on a journey and be put at risk.
Buried treasure thrills no hearts, throws no parties, wins no friends, buys no pleasure.
All he asks of you is
to accept that he has made you rich, and to be generous
with your own tales
spilling over from life's full cup.

---

[11]   Originally published in Woodward, Gooder and Pryce (2012: 96–7).

The house that Joseph built[12]

I took on an awkward job once,
To mend a clumsy house – I swear it had a squint
And broken back:
Walls askew, angles in an argument,
Almost every part of it untrue, at odds,
Going to ruin.

Make it beautiful he said,
Make it elegant he said,
Make it fit for a bride he said*,*
        upon her honeymoon.

To make it work
I had to love that property;
Each quirk and fault
I valued like my own design;
Each defect fixed with splice and peg
And blended wood, as if I'd always meant it.

Make it warm he said*,*
Make it comfortable he said,
Make it dry and safe enough he said,
        for a mother and her baby.

It taught me, this dumb house,
That being a craftsman is sometimes to embrace
The un-chosen task
And the failings of others,
To bring a generous expertise
Which mends, and makes a future.

Make it broad he said
Make it tall he said
Make it big enough he said
        for visitors to come and wonder.

Make it calm he said,
Make it still he said,
Make it cool he said
        For a corpse to sleep his way through Sabbath.

---

[12]   Originally published in Woodward, Gooder and Pryce (2013).

Patterns in words...[13]

In the garden,
Three prayers of terror: 'Let this cup pass';
Three prayers of trust: 'Your will be done';
Three prayers unsaid: his followers asleep.

In the darkness,
Three fearful treacheries: the kiss, the sword, the flight;
Three pious priestly rants: the truth unheard;
Three vehement denials: 'I do not know the man.'

In the morning,
Three unjust conspiracies: Pilate, priests and people;
Three handy props for mockery: the robe, the reed, the thorns;
Three furious steps to murder: first isolate your victim, next scorn, then the kill.

In the daylight,
Three filthy criminals: a cross for each;
Three painful hours of agony: the nails, the nakedness, the thirst;
Three tests of his obedience: to save himself, come down, defend his dignity.

In the end time,
Three witnesses of death: the wakened saints, centurion, the women standing;
Three powers to stifle life: the stone, the seal, the guards;
Three faithful friends to wonder: rich Joseph, clearing up the mess; and Magdalene,
                                        with the other Mary, both watching ...

---

[13]   Originally published in Woodward, Gooder and Pryce (2013).

References

Alves, Rubem A., *The Poet, The Warrior, The Prophet* (London: SCM Press, 1990)

Atwell, Robert (comp.), *Celebrating the Saints: Daily Spiritual Readings for the Calendar of the Church of England* (Norwich: Canterbury Press, 1998)

Barry, Patrick OSB, *Saint Benedict's Rule: A New Translation for Today* (Leominster: Gracewing/Ampleforth Abbey Press, 1997)

Brueggemann, Walter, *The Prophetic Imagination* (Philadelphia: Fortress Press, 1983)

Brueggemann, Walter, *Finally Comes the Poet: Daring Speech for Proclamation* (Minneapolis: Fortress Press, 1989)

Capps, Donald, *The Poet's Gift: Towards the Renewal of Pastoral Care* (Louisville, Kentucky: Westminster/John Knox Press, 1993)

Causley, Charles, *Collected Poems 1951-1997* (London: Macmillan, 1997)

Ceridwen, Manon, *Poems* (2013), available at http://manonceridwen.wordpress.com/category/poems

Church of England, *Common Worship* (London: Church House Publishing, 2000), available at http://www.churchofengland.org/prayer-worship/worship/texts/the-calendar/holydays

Culbertson, Philip, 'Explaining Men', in James B. Nelson and Sandra P. Longfellow, *Sexuality and the Sacred: Sources for Theological Reflection* (London: Mowbray, 1994, 183–94)

Davies, Cynthia and Saunders Davies (eds), *Euros Bowen: Priest-Poet/bardd-offeiriad* (Penarth: Church in Wales Publications, 1993)

Davis, Ellen E., *Proverbs, Ecclesiastes, and the Song of Songs* (Louisville, Kentucky: Westminster/John Knox Press, 2000)

Guite, Malcolm, *Faith, Hope and Poetry: Theology and the Poetic Imagination* (Farnham: Ashgate, 2010)

Hill, Geoffrey, *Collected Poems* (London: Viking, 1985)

Hill, Geoffrey, *Canaan* (London: Penguin, 1996)

Hill, Geoffrey, *The Orchards of Syon* (London: Penguin, 2002)

Housman, A.E., *A Shropshire Lad* (London: The Folio Society, 1986 [1896])

Kildea, Paul, *Benjamin Britten: A Life in the Twentieth Century* (London: Allen Lane, 2013)

McGough, Roger, *As Far As I Know* (London: Viking, 2012)

Mann, Rachel, *Poems* (2013) available at http://www.rachelmann.co.uk/pp001. shtml

Merton, Thomas, *The Collected Poems of Thomas Merton* (New York: New Directions, 1977)

Nelson, James, *The Intimate Connection: Male Sexuality, Masculine Sexuality* (London: SPCK, 1992)

Oliver, Mary, *Thirst* (Tarset: Bloodaxe, 2007)

Oliver, Mary, *Red Bird* (Tarset: Bloodaxe, 2008)

O'Regan, Tariq with Mark Pryce, 'Bring rest, sweet, dreaming child' (London: Novello, 2004)

O'Siadhail, Micheal, *Poems 1975-1995* (Newcastle: Bloodaxe, 1999)

Pattison, Stephen, *A Critique of Pastoral Care* [3rd edition] (London: SCM Press, 2000)

Pattison, Stephen with James Woodward, *A Vision of Pastoral Theology* (Edinburgh: Contact Pastoral, 1994)

Plath, Sylvia, *Ariel* (London: Faber and Faber, 1965)

Pryce, Mark, *Finding a Voice: Men, Women and the Community of the Church* (London: SCM Press, 1996)

Pryce, Mark, *Literary Companion to the Lectionary* (London: SPCK/Fortress, 2001)

Pryce, Mark, *Literary Companion for Festivals* (London: SPCK/Fortress, 2003)

Quash, Ben, 'Real Enactment: The Role of Drama in the Theology of Urs von Balthasar', in Trevor A. Hart and Steven R. Guthrie, *Faithful Performances: Enacting Christian Tradition* (Aldershot: Ashgate, 2007) 13–32

Rahner, Hugo, *Man at Play; Or Did You Ever Practice Eutrapelia?* Translated by Brian Battershaw and Edward Quinn (London: Burns & Oates, 1965)

Rahner, Karl, 'Poetry and the Christian', in *Theological Investigations*, trans. K. Smyth; vol. IV [1966] (London: Darton, Longman & Todd, 1982) 357–67

Raine, Kathleen, *The Land Unknown: Chapters of Autobiography* (New York: George Braziller, 1975)

Rowell, Geoffrey, Kenneth Stevenson and Rowan Williams (compilers), *Love's Redeeming Work: The Anglican Quest for Holiness* (Oxford: Oxford University Press, 2001)

Scott, David, *A Quiet Gathering* (Newcastle: Bloodaxe, 1984)

Scott, David, *Playing for England* (Newcastle: Bloodaxe, 1989)

Slee, Nicola and Helen Cameron, 'Peering into the Shadows or Foregrounding the Feminine? Feminist rewritings of the Parable of the Prodigal', *Practical Theology* (forthcoming)

Spender, Stephen, *Dolphins* (London: Faber & Faber, 1994)

Symmons Roberts, Michael, *Corpus* (London: Cape, 2004)

Symmons Roberts, Michael, *Drysalter* (London: Cape, 2013)

Thomas, R.S., *Collected Poems 1945–1990* (London: J.M. Dent, 1993)

Tristam, Br. SSF (ed.), *Exciting Holiness: Collects and Readings for Festivals and Lesser Festivals of the Church of England* (Norwich: Canterbury Press, 1997)

Veling, Terry A., *Practical Theology 'On Earth as It Is in Heaven'* (Maryknoll, New York: Orbis Books, 2005)

Williams, Rowan, *On Christian Theology* (Oxford: Blackwell, 2000)

Williams, Rowan, *Remembering Jerusalem* (Oxford: The Perpetua Press, 2001)

Williams, Rowan, *Headwaters* (Oxford: The Perpetua Press, 2008)

Woodward, James, Paula Gooder and Mark Pryce, *Journeying with Mark* (London: SPCK, 2011)

Woodward, James, Paula Gooder and Mark Pryce, *Journeying with Luke* (London: SPCK, 2012)

Woodward, James, Paula Gooder and Mark Pryce, *Journeying with Matthew* (London: SPCK, 2013)

Chapter 4

Where Poems Come From: Spirituality, Emotion and *Poiesis*

Eleanor Nesbitt

Preamble

After sharing some thoughts on how poetry, spirituality and emotion are related, I will disclose something of the poetic influences on my own writing. This brings me to an examination of how I understand the interplay of crafting and inspiration: in other words, I will attempt to unravel my own practice. Thoughts on resonances and borrowings morph into comment on luminous poetry and resplendent doubt. Exploration of formative, cross-cultural influences on what I write and consistencies with my Quaker faith preface my focus on the poems that presented themselves for inclusion in the present volume.

'Spirituality' is an abstraction, two removes (via the adjective 'spiritual') from spirit. 'Spiritual' (except as the outpouring of Black American bondage, yearning and faith) has lost the vigour of its etymological cousin 'spirited', and of 'spirit' itself (whether ghostly or alcoholic). 'Spirituality', like 'inspiration', somehow lacks this earlier energy. And for most people (unless they are at home in a Christian milieu and mindset) the words 'Holy Spirit', like 'Holy Ghost', denote nothing lively or relevant. Yet the English language has no more copious or apt word than 'spirituality' for the quality or dimension of humanity that it suggests – a dimension that overlaps with human responses to beauty, and with moral insights.

I say all this while, contrarily, also empathising with Philip Pullman's protest:

> I think that matter is quite extraordinary and wonderful and mysterious enough, without adding something called spirit to it; in fact any talk about *the spiritual*

> makes me a little uneasy. When I hear such utterances as 'My spiritual journey',
> or 'I'm spiritual but not religious', or 'So-and-so is a deeply spiritual person …
> my reaction is a visceral one. I pull back almost physically. (2011: 251)

My persistence in using this possibly superfluous, sometimes insipid, and – to some readers – abhorrent word 'spirituality' stems from the experience that it does carry meaning for plenty of people, and from the sense that what I mean by it and what they understand by it seem to coincide or at least to overlap. Among others, late twentieth-century and early twenty-first-century religious educationists' discussions have focused on 'spiritual development' and spirituality. Aspects that they identify include both moral and aesthetic awareness and the capacity for 'awe and wonder', areas of experience that have so often found distinctive expression by poets.

Poetry and spirituality are linked, and this is undergirded by etymology, as (more generally and concretely) *poiesis* – the Greeks' word two and a half millennia ago for doing and making, and hence for poems, poetry, poesy – depends totally upon our life-breath (the Romans' *spiritus*). So, poems are conceived in the union of the spiritual (especially as sensitivity to the good and beautiful) and the creative, a unity that is rooted in activity as biologically basic as breathing and doing. This wellspring feeds words: word is not there in its beginning, and the wellspring sustains also deep silences and wordless musical expression. As the verb for doing, the Greek verb *poiein* embraces making but is not confined to it. It has the energy of action, of implementation, as in Matthew 7: 24–7.

The creative surge behind the action is emotion, not necessarily an emotion that is as specific as joy, sorrow, anger and the rest, but it is certainly (as the word emotion's Latin origins suggest) a 'moving out' from a stirring within. Nor is religiously or spiritually infused poetry prompted by some special type of emotion. Indeed, as sociologists of religion, Ole Riis and Linda Woodhead, have pointed out, '[a]*ny* emotion can be religious: not only awe and serenity, but grief, ecstasy, anxiety, self-righteousness, and so on' (2010: 54).

Turning from sociologists to poets, what is clear is that emotion, certainly in the sense of particular emotions, immediately connects us with poetry's histories. Wendy Cope, the contemporary British poet, observed dryly that 'Sometimes poetry is emotion recollected in a highly emotional state' (1992: 47). In so doing, she assumed that her readers and hearers already understood, with William Wordsworth, that 'poetry is the spontaneous overflow of powerful feelings: it takes its origin from emotion recollected in tranquillity' (1800). Cope must have expected her readers to think of Wordsworth, at peace on his couch, remembering his tumultuous response to the host of dancing daffodils. Maybe the poet R.S. Thomas, too, had Wordsworth's dictum in mind when, in his poem entitled 'Don't Ask me', he stated 'Poetry is that / which arrives at the intellect / by way of the heart' (2004: 355).

Talk of emotion in relation to poetry takes me to 'The Birth of Poetry', a painting by Kattingeri Krishna Hebbar, a celebrated twentieth-century artist from the Indian state of Karnataka (see http://www.artintaglio.in/ViewProdDetails. jsp?cateId=13&ProdId=2890 accessed 26 April 2013). A reproduction of 'The Birth of Poetry' hung on the wall of my colleague Kamla Sawhney's room in the boarding school in Naini Tal, in Uttarakhand state, in the Himalayan foothills where she and I both taught in the mid-1970s. Hebbar's inspiration was the incident that stirred Valmiki, a renowned sage, to compose the Ramayana. On seeing a hunter's arrow kill a bird in the act of making love, Valmiki felt keenly for the grieving mate. This pang was the start of his prodigious epic, a saga that has the standing of scripture for hundreds of millions of Hindus.

My Multiple Inheritance

It is no accident that a European (indeed a British) trail of connections (Europe's classical languages, William Wordsworth, Wendy Cope) should converge with an Indian thought association when I think about emotion and poetry, and about poetry and its origination. India is a strong thread in who I am, and has been for the past four decades, through my periods of literally being there (starting with that stint in the 1970s), as well as by virtue of being, through marriage, part of a Punjabi family. Professionally, too, I have been caught up, as an academic for over 30 years, in interpreting the religious/cultural traditions of South Asia (see e.g. Jackson and Nesbitt, 1993; Nesbitt and Kaur, 1999; Nesbitt, 2005). In the main I have been engaging with various Hindu and Sikh communities, and especially with their religious activities in a period of rapid social change.

So Hindu and Sikh images stir me to write while, at the same time, my European roots are, as a onetime classicist, in Greece and Rome as well as in my very Church of England childhood of daily bible-reading and weekly matins. The poem 'In Smethwick Rolfe Street' (below) is one superficially light-hearted articulation of a recurrent dilemma, namely what to edit out and what to elaborate for hearers and readers whose funds of cultural image and imagination may overlap but only in part. I challenge the monopolised niche status of 'ethnic minority' poets. The footnoting is a rather tongue-in-cheek allusion to my usual genre, articles for peer reviewed journals. Why did I footnote Indic words, rather than 'Adlestrop' or, indeed, 'Smethwick'? My assumptions about who reads what, may, I know, be misplaced.

My dilemma is of course far from peculiar: it is typical of contemporary social diversity, the 'modern plurality' that increasingly characterises the experience of individuals and groups (Skeie, 1995), a modern plurality that I characterise elsewhere as a plural spirituality (Nesbitt, 2003). Moreover, our 'emotional regimes' (Riis and Woodhead, 2010: 10–12, 47–51), that were once (or so it is easy to imagine) more or less bounded zones of cultural behaviour, free-standing belief systems, now repeatedly impinge, thanks to migration and travel, and they also interact within individuals. I realise, and especially after the publication of the UK census 2011 statistics on the increasing number of ethnically mixed individuals, how anachronistic it is to feel that a multiple heritage is unusual or problematic.

While in this trans-cultural vein, I am reminded of the dual role of verse, in its many social contexts. It whispers and it cries aloud as the subversive voice, the articulation of doubt, disbelief and protest, often dismissing sacred convention or received wisdom. And (in due course) the same verse (the Hebrew psalms, the book of Job, the Guru Granth Sahib) comes to reign as canon. Seeing how, in such different times and places, protest can mellow into orthodoxy, and impulse can harden into institution, points up every generation's need for new poems to spring and spark and spur.

Of Crafting and Inspiration

In drafting this chapter I have a sense of *déjà vu*, as the challenge recalls a task required of me some years previously as a university teacher. After years of carrying out ethnographic fieldwork (studies involving participant observation and semi-structured interviews) I was required formally to train graduate students in research methods, and in particular to introduce them to a qualitative approach. Before they embarked on their fieldwork they needed to be briefed about key ideas that underpin empirical research and the practical procedures that they could enlist in finding answers to the research questions which they had very carefully to design. In keeping with anthropological tradition I encouraged successive cohorts of students to find ways of making the familiar strange as well as making the strange familiar (Geertz, 1973: 215). The popular distancing device of imagining oneself as a Martian reporting on a visit to planet Earth subsequently found expression in my poem 'Earthling Religion' (see below). However, the start of my own decades of fieldwork had pre-dated much of my attention to methodological principles, and also pre-dated the obligatory research methods courses, that took shape during my time as a university teacher. An unflinchingly critical analysis of how I had carried out my own studies was integral to setting out a framework for good practice and for engaging successive cohorts of students with questions about validity. In much the same way, I had been writing poems for decades before trying to identify or discuss stages in the creative process, or characterising the literary context for my own writing.

Some lines of Théophile Gautier (1811–1872) from his poem, 'L'Art', during my school study of French Romantic poets had, however, sown seeds of inquisitiveness about an intrinsic tension, or balance, between poetry's elusive inspiration and its wordsmithing through the discipline of poesy. Gautier too was bound into a culture that connected him, often self-consciously, with classical Greece:

> Point de contraintes fausses!
> Mais que pour marcher droit
> Tu chausses, Muse, un cothurne étroit. (1872: 131)

Gautier's lines make me, ever the literalist, smile, as I cannot think of a falser constraint for poems than having to wear a tight *cothurna*, the sort of boot worn by actors of Greek tragedy, or adopting the medium of enamel rather than water colour! Gautier's boot appears in my mind's eye as I read Ray Muna's haiku:

Like size zero scarlet jeans
Or stiletto shoes with trim bright buckles
Haikus pinch my tender form.[1]

In my own case, the crafting (applying at least the vestiges of a discipline) is often unconscious (not at all like coaxing or ramming my feet into unyielding or ridiculously inappropriate footwear), and so poetic devices and details in my poems have sometimes been only pointed out to me afterwards by others. The present task of writing reflectively for this volume impels me to be more aware of my crafting, as well as of the poems' sources, and so (I hope) it leads to my honing the requisite skills through sharing my reflections with readers. In a Radio 4 interview in 2012 the novelist and bioethicist, Alexander McCall-Smith, described how his stories of a lady detective in Botswana come to him, spontaneously, without prior planning. I identified with him in his stated reluctance to investigate the mysterious process further, in case he ceased to be able to write.

At the same time, a glance through my work discloses a recurrent preoccupation, since at least the 1980s, with the springs of creativity. My fascination with this mystery finds expression in analogy and metaphor, and in the parallel with the experience of being 'called' to stand up and to offer what we Quakers call 'spoken ministry' in our Meetings for Worship ('In Quaker Meeting', see below). Fishing in the sea ('Fisherman', Nesbitt, 1999: 28) provided one set of images for poetry-writing, and the potter's craft suggested another: 'Poems / Pummelled like lumpen clay, / Hollowed and moulded. Words / Wheel-turned and fired...' ('Hobby Misheard', Nesbitt, 1999: 26). Another poem 'Creation' (Nesbitt 1999: 27) highlighted how differently different poems seem to arrive, with some coming 'sudden, / Swift, sure as the fall / Of ripened fruit' whereas others were 'averse / To being born, verses / Reluctant, needing to be coaxed, / Encouraged, drawn out slowly'. In this poem, and from my poems on this theme collectively, what emerges is a recognition of both effort and givenness, crafting and channelling, enamelling as well as doodling, constraining footwear as well as bare feet. More and more clearly I acknowledge the effect of being in a succession, a poetic tradition.

It is my respect for a creative experience that continues to surprise me that has led to my choosing for the present volume four poems that are concerned with

---

[1]   Unpublished poem, privately circulated as Dear (2012).

poetic creation. In this tendency to set down poetically something of the creative process, I realise of course that I am not alone: for example, two contemporary poets, Gwyneth Lewis and Angela Topping, have teased out the same theme in, respectively, 'How to Capture a Poem' (Topping, 2009: 20) and 'How to Knit a Poem' (Lewis, no date: 26). Also, one programme of *Poetry Please* (BBC Radio 4) was devoted to the theme of poets, Ted Hughes and Carol Ann Duffy among them, writing about writing poetry (15 April 2007). Lewis instructs us to: 'Tie a loop in nothing', 'It's thought in action. It redeems odd corners of disposable time …' Topping's poem ends:

> Release it. It has nothing more to do
> with you. You're no more its owner
> than you hold the wind. Never expect gratitude.

That chimes with my experience too. Capturing, yes, though often it's the poem that captures me, as with ministry in a Quaker Meeting for Worship:

> Silence and clean white paper are alike receptive.
> The urgency, the imperative to write are as directive
> As feeling called to stand.[2]

Although the poem does not allude to the part that the Meeting, qua gathering of fellow seekers, may play in feeling prompted to 'minister', I must not omit my 'faith community' when reflecting on both inspiration and crafting. Pondering spirituality makes me acknowledge the way in which my life has been enriched by being part of a community of Quakers. I am indebted particularly to the companionship of those who gather week by week in the Quaker meeting house in Coventry. In the tradition of Quakers in Britain Yearly Meeting of the Religious Society of Friends (Quakers), unlike the more vocal 'programmed meetings' of Quakers in many other countries, we come together in silence each week for the experiment that is Quaker Meeting for Worship.

Likewise, the sense of being one of a mutually supportive band of poets has sustained me, and here I refer to the Gemini Poets (see Florance and Nesbitt, 2011)

---

[2]   'In Quaker Meeting' (see below) was first published in Nesbitt (1999: 26).

and to my local group, the Coventry Live Poets (the context for my poem 'Suggestions' below), as well as to the Diviners. In addition to being upheld by groups of fellow poets who value each other, who share their problems and successes as well as their poems, and who offer friendly criticism of each other's work, these groups, no less than my Quaker meeting, feel like safe spaces in which to share inklings of life's meaning, and its minutiae and magnitude.

With regard to crafting: concentration as I draft and patient, unwavering, alert listening to the lines as I repeatedly reread them are central. If possible I read aloud. I listen for patterning and surprise. I notice, as if in someone else's composition, the metre, alliteration, assonance, and any onomatopoeia. Lines may call for tweaking or for re-sequencing. I may devote time to experimentally repositioning the line breaks. The surprise most often comes in the final line or near the beginning, and may be no more than an ironic turn of phrase. I am learning the discipline of excising words and lines that are superfluous, and here the poetry groups are helping to steel me. Sometimes it is the prized last line that has to be sacrificed.

The musicality of verse is important to me. If my verses were read to someone with no knowledge of English, would the words sound any more beautiful or affective than a shopping list or a railway announcement? My hunch is that poetry must carry a musicality which leaves the listener in no doubt that what she is hearing is poetry. As Newey reminded readers of the *Guardian*, 'poetry … is different from song precisely because it carries its own music within it. Where song lyrics are written to function within a musical frame, poetry is framed in silence (2012).' Poetry cannot rely on the accompaniment of music for its own musicality.

Yes, poetry is framed in silence, but the spaces that allow for the needful concentration on drafting, listening, listening, drafting are not timetabled and need not be silent. In my own case I realise that buses and trains have birthed many of my poems, one of them 'Elephanta' (see below). Clearly, if poems have the momentum to take shape even on a jolting, swerving, overflowing, rowdy Indian bus, with no elbow room and not a second of quiet, it is not the absence of surrounding activity and noise that is a prerequisite but more likely the isolation from competing demands on one's time and attention: buses and trains, like airports, afford 'that solitude that crowds allow' (see 'Poems', below).

Resonances and Borrowings

As I examine my own output I realise increasingly how interconnected its content is both with contemporary poets and with poets of previous generations. Only some years after writing a poem entitled 'The Bush' (Florance and Nesbitt, 2011: 90), with its implicit reference to chapter 3 of the book of Exodus, did I read Elizabeth Barrett Browning's words:

> But only he who sees, takes off his shoes –
> The rest sit round it and pluck blackberries. (1917, 'Aurora Leigh' VII 1)

It is unfailingly exciting to realise that a celebrated poet has entertained a thought or used an image similar to something in one's own writing. Given that until recent decades almost all mother-tongue speakers of English were, like myself, brought up with biblical narrative (and a substantial minority of them with Greek and Latin literature too) such inter-connections are unsurprising. As well as retrospectively seeing links back to earlier poets, on occasion, I find that a more established contemporary's poems stir mine to life. I recall, at a Coventry meeting of the Punjab Research Group, hearing the Punjabi poet Amarjit Chandan (see, for example, 2005) reading a poem about his sense of exile as an emigrant from Punjab, and then how my own poem 'Exile' (Nesbitt, 1999: 14) surfaced the next day. The emotion behind 'Exile' was my own regret at being so distanced, not from a literal homeland (as in Chandan's case and in the case of so many immigrant poets), but from the religious certainties of my own forebears. His poem of migration as exile drew out mine. And as I read through my poem I came to know myself better. Only more recently have I wondered whether Matthew Arnold's 'long withdrawing roar' of the faith that had once encircled the world had also called my poem into existence ('Dover Beach' in Ricks, 1999: 453–4).[3]

Often, however, I am fully aware at the time of writing that an earlier poet's phrase is infiltrating something I am writing. So, in composing 'For Rowan' (Florance and Nesbitt, 2011: 54) the impetus was Archbishop Rowan Williams quoting, in a television interview, the line from Act 1 scene iv of Shakespeare's

---

[3]   Available at http://www.victorianweb.org/authors/arnold/writings/doverbeach.html Accessed 27 April 2013.

King Lear, 'Who is it that can tell me who I am?' My response echoed some translated words from the Greek poet Pindar (sixth century BCE) that I had put up on my wall as an undergraduate student of Greek: *skias onar anthropos* 'man, the dream of a shadow'. They come from lines of Pindar's eighth Pythian ode that have been translated as:

> Man's life is a day. What is he?
> What is he not? A shadow in a dream
> Is man… (Bowra 1969: 237)

Only some years after writing my poem did I realise, with a tingle, that the Fool's answer to the king's question is 'Lear's shadow'.

From the poets of classical Greece and Rome, it has always been Lucretius, the non-theist, who speaks to me most powerfully, but I have yet to detect any echo of his mighty, exquisitely detailed, highly alliterative *De Rerum Natura*[4] in any line of mine. In the case of Lucretius it is the brutal honesty of his iconoclastic personality combined with the beauty of his torrents of images, plus the ring of his syllables with their shameless crescendos of alliteration, that catch my imagination. With Pindar's fragment it is the luminosity of an eventual enlightenment that captured me as an 18-year-old: *lampron phengos epesti kai meilichos aion*: 'a bright light comes and a gentle age'.[5]

Luminosity characterises many of the poems that stay in my memory, poems intimating George Herbert's 'heaven in ordinarie' (1857), William Blake's 'world in a grain of sand… eternity in an hour' (1952: 171). Francis Thompson's exhortation, 'Turn but a stone and start a wing' (1917: 425, 'The Kingdom of God') chimes with Gerard Manley Hopkins' affirmation that 'The world is charged with the grandeur of God / It will flame out, like shining from shook foil' ('God's grandeur' in Gardner and MacKenzie, 1970: 66). Such poems are lit from within, from that 'bright unsullied sky', perhaps, that Emily Brontë found within herself ('To Imagination').[6]

Malcolm Guite's study, *Faith, Hope and Poetry*, sensitively and authoritatively traces the lineages of 'understanding light' (2010: 75–102), 'visions of the invisible'

---

[4]   The Nature of the Universe; see Latham (1951).

[5]   Bowra's rendering is 'Shining life is on earth / And life is sweet as honey (1969: 237).

[6]   Available at http://www.online-literature.com/bronte/1365/ Accessed 27 April 2013.

(2010: 125–44), 'doubting faith' and 'transfigured vision' (2010: 179–200), but from these lineages the voices of women are strangely absent. On my own path I have relished the companionship of many women. Spanning the millennia Sappho (who in the seventh century BCE. first coined bittersweet, or at least 'sweet-bitter', *glukupikron*)[7] meets in my mind's eye with Elizabeth Barrett Browning and with Emily Brontë, whose poem 'No coward soul is mine'[8] I encountered as one of the hymns in *Songs of Praise* that we sang in our morning school assembly. Among this inspiring band of women poets, the work of U.A. Fanthorpe (2010), the twentieth-century Quaker poet, has a special magnetism for me.

Revisiting my own poem 'In Quaker Meeting' reminded me to reread two great Quaker poems: U.A. Fanthorpe's 'Friends' Meeting House, Frenchay, Bristol' (2010: 272) and Sibyl Ruth's 'A Song of Jean' (2008: 34). Fanthorpe speaks of the 'Rare herb of silence, through which the Word comes.' Ruth evokes the spoken ministry of Jean, a commanding woman whose faculties are failing in old age. With her rousing ministry 'She drives away false peace, awakens us.' Among Quaker poets, who include, separated by a century and an ocean, John Greanleaf Whittier (2009) and Philip Gross (2009, 2011), I find myself especially revisiting Quaker women poets Stevie Krayer (2004) and R.V. Bailey (2004, 2010, 2012), and returning to Margaret Crompton's evocation of a hide in a bird sanctuary 'Quiet as a Quaker meeting / Hide by the bird rich lake'. The poem closes with 'a glimpse of God / in the hide of our hearts' ('Sunday Birding').[9]

Here, before articulating something of my own faith, I must pay tribute to birds. Wherever I have lived, their voices have reminded me that human activities are only one of the dramas unfolding each day. Other species have other scripts. And their voices prevent any day from being humdrum. My thoughts turn to the Indian poet-rishi Valmiki's bereaved *kraunca* bird (probably – although Hebbar's painting does not suggest this – a sarus crane, Grus Antigone). Nearer home are Shelley's skylark (Heaney and Hughes, 1982: 316–8),[10] John Keats's nightingale

---

[7] For the Greek verse see Page (1968: 122). Online discussion of the effect of the English word's reversal of Sappho's 'sweet-bitter' includes http://josephpaulmatthews. blogspot.co.uk/2012/05/glukupikron.html Accessed 27 April 2013.

[8] Available at http://www.online-literature.com/bronte/1352/ Accessed 27 April 2013.

[9] Unpublished poem, privately circulated in Dear (2012).

[10] 'To a Skylark' available at http://www.poetryfoundation.org/poem/174413 Accessed 27 April 2013.

(Ricks, 1999: 403–4),[11] Thomas Hardy's 'darkling thrush' (Heaney and Hughes, 1982: 120–21),[12] Gerard Manley Hopkins's 'dapple-dawn-drawn Falcon' ('The Windhover', Gardner and MacKenzie 1970, 69) and woodlark (Heaney and Hughes, 1982: 470–71), Edward Thomas's owl (Heaney and Hughes, 1982: 330–31) and 'speculating rooks' ('Thaw' in Ricks, 1999: 542),[13] as well as Ted Hughes's 'Crow and the Birds' (Schmidt, 1999: 507) and the mighty roll call of massed birds in David Morley's 'Chorus',[14] and that blackbird that sang briefly one June afternoon at Adlestrop.[15] I hear myself reiterating 'I hope I never understand the birds' (Nesbitt, 1999: 22).

My Own 'Faith'

'I hope I never understand the birds' were the last words of a poem, 'Easter', that I wrote in India in about 1975:

> I could believe, but words
> All too precise entomb
> The gladness …
> At least the song of birds
> Remains mysterious. Still
> We, the word-alert, can thrill
> To thrush and lark,
> Our minds unstirred
> To faithless protest.

---

[11]   'Ode to a Nightingale' available at http://www.poetryfoundation.org/poem/173744 Accessed 27 April 2013.

[12]   'The Darkling Thrush' available at http://www.poetryfoundation.org/poem/173590 Accessed 27 April 2013.

[13]   'Thaw' available at http://www.matthewhollis.com/publications/edwardthomas.php Accessed 2 May 2013.

[14]   'Chorus' available at www.wolfmagazine.co.uk/22poem2.php Accessed 3 May 2013.

[15]   'Adlestrop' available at http://www.poemhunter.com/poem/adlestrop Accessed 15 October 2012.

So, in my heading for this section I have enclosed 'faith' in speech marks. They signal a compound unease. First, there is my caution, stemming from years of puzzling, as a religious studies/religious education person, over appropriate terminology. 'Religion', 'belief', 'creed', 'worldview', 'tradition', 'faith', 'stance' – all these terms have their histories, connotations and limitations. The problematic character of a Protestant Christian assumption that belief (creed, conviction) is so basic to 'religion' as to be synonymous with it calls for caution. Second, there is my respect for a word that encompasses trust and confidence as well as systematised doctrine and world religions. Clearly 'faith' is an embracing, inclusive word that may call for some pinning down in particular contexts. Third, and most crucially, I have to acknowledge that my own 'faith' is in large measure questioning and doubt, rejection and resistance.

Here I feel a grateful connectedness to my English heritage of doubting poets: Thomas Hardy, Matthew Arnold, Philip Larkin and so many more. One after another has voiced a faith which is doubt and doubt which is faith, an integrity that cuts through hypocrisy and dispenses with comforting reassurances. And it is through the deepest doubting that faith, unconstrained by theological defining, beckons. Tennyson suggested 'There lives more faith in honest doubt / Believe me, than in half the creeds' ('In Memoriam' xcvi, no date).

For Quakers (or Friends), and particularly for my own community, the twentieth- and twenty-first-century Quakers of Britain Yearly Meeting, uncertainty and questioning are basic. But Quakers' core, the Meeting for Worship, also presupposes and nurtures reverence.

The shared practice of Meeting for Worship, a (usually) weekly space for listening and waiting in the company of other Friends, underpins the questing and the social activism (Durham, 2011). This practice of listening underlies the cultivation of openness to others' insights and preoccupations that I have needed in my years of fieldwork, listening to Hindus, Sikhs, and Christians of many ethnic and denominational backgrounds. Moreover, the Quaker valuing of experience and of living experimentally is consistent with conducting research and encouraging students in their research. Waiting and listening are very much part of my experience as both ethnographer and poet: one may wait for weeks, months or years for the germination of a poem, or be prepared to welcome, discerningly, several in quick succession. Listening out for turns of phrase is rewarded too by opening sentences; so often it is these given words that spark off the rest of a poem. 'Healing', 'Elephanta', 'Shraddh', 'In Quaker Meeting' and 'Poems' all began in this way. So too does some of my Quaker ministry. Less often, some printed words draw out a poem, as in 'This entrance ...' (below) and 'In Holland and Barratt' (Florance and Nesbitt, 2011: 37). On another occasion a sound is the start: this was the case with 'Midlands snowfall' as the muffled crunch-cum-squeak of treading ice overlaid by fresh snow set me searching for a word and lighting on 'thwock', courtesy of Ian Florance's poem 'Churchill's Funeral 2003' (Florance and Nesbitt, 2011: 28).

Passing years have brought a growing sense of gratitude for the unity between not only my experience as a Quaker and as a poet but also between both these dimensions of my life and my professional and academic work. Intellectually, this has stirred me to tease out the inter-connections between being a Quaker and being an ethnographer (Nesbitt, 2002), between being a Quaker and conducting research in Hindu and Sikh Studies (2010) and between my poems and scholarly convention in theology and religious studies.

By ethnography I mean the processes of designing, conducting and reporting research that draws much of its data from fieldwork – fieldwork which is as far as possible an immersion in a community's life, although interviews too play a part (Nesbitt, 2006). Such interviews are often quite loosely structured so as to allow individuals space to articulate what is of importance to them, rather than being constricted by wording arising from the researcher's agenda. Like Jane Piirto (2002) I can see a place in the ethnographic process for responses in poetry as well as prose. My poems 'Glastonbury', 'Elephanta' and 'In Smethwick Rolfe Street' (in this volume) enable me to reflect on the 'layering' of sacred space (Bowman, 2011) as well as to examine further the element of transparency and reflexivity in conducting and reporting research into religious places, communities and behaviour.

Cliché is a poet's downfall, as too is a straining of colloquial idiom in order to fit self-imposed patterns of metre or rhyme. Similarly, Quakers aspire to the rejection of any unquestioning observance of ritual and repetition of creedal statements. But, being human, they have fashioned their own familiar terminology and routines. Whether I am engaging with Quaker activity or with writing or critiquing poetry, I am on that tightrope between honoured form and expressive freedom, a tightrope on which, like truth, it is best not to stand still for too long.

The Quaker way originated in Christianity, as one of many Protestant movements in turbulent seventeenth-century England. My biblical and liturgical nurture in the Church of England sustains my Quaker experience with a stronger continuity than would be the case if I had instead embarked on a Hindu- or Buddhist-derived spiritual path. The teaching of Jesus underpins *Quaker Faith and Practice* (Britain Yearly Meeting of the Religious Society of Friends [Quakers] in Britain, 2008). In keeping with our understanding of the purpose and manner of Jesus of Nazareth, Quakers are reminded of the need to be grounded in the cluster of values at the heart of our 'Testimonies': simplicity, truth, justice/equality, peace, and – increasingly separated out as an explicit testimony – sustainability and care for the environment. Writing this piece leaves me with the challenge to examine whether or not my poems express any of these values. My hope is that they do.

At the same time, perhaps to a unique degree among bodies with a Christian foundation, the Quaker way affirms the individual in spiritual journeying through and with 'other' faiths (Pym, 2000; Nesbitt, 2003). Inter-spirituality and dual belonging pose intellectual puzzles but do not run counter to an essentially inclusive Quaker approach. Grounded in their engagement with individuals of diverse cultural and philosophical traditions, the writings of the philosopher of religions John Hick (1999), who became a Quaker in his later years, and the formerly Catholic (now Protestant) theologian Perry Schmidt-Leukel (2009) encourage my own adventure.

The sense of 'union' ('In Quaker Meeting'), 'at-oneness' ('Healing') and harmony with nature surfaces in many of my poems and is consistent with my experience of Quaker Meeting for Worship. It is in line too with Indic intuitions. In the 'humming' and 'homing through stillness' ('Healing') I detect the vibration of the mantra syllable 'om', and the monistic understanding of Shankara – 'the ancient sage's certainty / That all are one' ('Shraddh').

Twenty-one Poems

My contribution to this volume offers 21 of my poems. Hope and healing, place and time, and poetic creation are themes connecting many of them. Some of the poems are bursting with questions – insistent questions about poetry and about

'God'. Others spring, less rhetorically and more descriptively, from the same search.

Hope and healing are illustrated by 'Prayer', 'Healing' and 'Theodicy', and I reproduce these poems because some readers say that they have found them supportive. 'This is my day' came out of an early morning meditation and was broadcast by Radio 4 in a programme presented by the Diviners. 'Prayer', the earliest, and the briefest of my contributions to this volume, comes from my time in India in the 1970s. It is associated in my memory with a professor of Urdu in Delhi University. For 'Healing' the starting point was a dismaying statement by my yoga teacher, a friend in Coventry Quaker Meeting. 'Theodicy' came, like a passage of dictation, early one morning at the point when my months of chemotherapy for breast cancer had ended and I was about to commence both radiotherapy and full-time work. Throughout the seven months of my sick leave I had reflected and journalled and hoped to occupy my unplanned leisure in writing poetry. Not a line. Then 'Theodicy' arrived with a strong impulse to share it and a sense that it was written on behalf of others, rather than its detail recounting what I myself had experienced: I had not experienced the sting of hurtful words which the poem mentions.

More whimsically, I have included 'Examination question' (from Askari et al. 2002), 'The person you are calling' and 'Earthling Religion'. 'Earthling Religion' owes its existence not only to anthropological theory but, more immediately, to a poetry workshop at Woodbrooke Quaker Study Centre, Birmingham that was led by Quaker poets R.V. Bailey and Stevie Krayer.

Four of the seven poems concerned with place and time set on record a transformative, stirring conjunction of time and place, two in the UK (a pilgrimage place and a railway station), and two in India (a cave temple frequented by tourists and a seashore where worship connects the living and their forefathers). Yet in two of these cases ('Glastonbury' and 'Elephanta') it was a similar emotional high in subsequent locations that precipitated the poems.

So, 'Glastonbury' came through on my return from Easedale Tarn (which itself found expression in 'Excelsior' (Nesbitt 1999: 8). Each of the four poems arose from a powerful sense of place – in Glastonbury almost an out of the body transport. On rereading, I recognise that my poem is also an oblique contribution to the insider/outsider debate in religious studies (Arweck and Stringer, 2002).

'Elephanta' was precipitated by a subsequent visit to India's reputedly wealthiest temple, at Tirupati in Andhra Pradesh, some days after my excursion to the island of Elephanta.

The minor epiphany in 'In Smethwick Rolfe Street' occurred, as with Edward Thomas's 'Adlestrop', in a little-known British railway station. Much as Smethwick brings into sharp focus the convergence of Punjabi and English residents, so too in my head Edward Thomas came into contact with the recently feted Punjabi-origin poet, Daljit Nagra (2007). New Commonwealth writing and England's literature seemed to be converging. Some sense of incongruity forced itself out into the open in half-rhymes and echoes: *kirtan*/curtain etc. Beneath the humour (the deliberate pedantry of footnoting, for example) are urgent questions: What is it that makes ground sacred? Is the UK's diverse society a jigsaw of separate pieces (ethnic groups, religious communities, languages) or indivisible, albeit subtly 'marbled' (Eck, 2000: 135)?

When 'Elephanta' forced itself on me on that Indian bus, I was unaware of any intertextual clues. The words 'broken stone' were certainly not consciously derived from T.S. Eliot's 'The Hollow Men' (1963: 77). But I was quickly aware of the poem's betrayal of personal autobiography and spiritual angst. In my mind's eye was the complex of cave temples, desecrated by fifteenth-century Portuguese sailors who used the bas-reliefs of deities for target practice. In particular, the damaged sculpture of Nataraja, Shiva as dancer of the cosmic dance, claimed my attention. When a Hindu poet translated my poem into Hindi, he interpreted my words 'last of a line' as meaning last in the queue to receive the sacraments. What I had meant was either that I had no children or that others coming after me would not share the ancestral acceptance of Christian doctrine. Sad though I am that, in the two decades since writing 'Elephanta', the adjective 'awesome' has become as trivialised and overused as 'awful' already was in my youth, I have not reworded the last line.

'Shraddh' is less condensed than the other poems. Possibly it is a work in progress: as such it merits a place in my attempt to unravel the way in which I write poems/the way in which poems arrive. As an enquiring traveller, and until the previous month a teacher in north India, I had first visited the South Indian Hindu place of pilgrimage, Rameshwaram, in 1977. I had marvelled at its place in the vast geography of the North Indian poet Valmiki's Ramayana epic. This was where, 3,000 kilometres from Punjab, he described an army of animals, headed by the monkey-commander, the god Hanuman, laying stepping stones (the Ram Setu, formerly known as Adam's Bridge) to connect the Indian mainland with Lanka (now Sri Lanka) with the purpose of rescuing Sita (wife of the god-king Rama) from imprisonment by her abductor, the demon-king Ravana. I had stood in the small temple that purportedly marks the spot where Rama had stood before crossing the bridge to Lanka.

In 1991 I returned, with my husband, a Punjabi Hindu who had never before visited the great temples of South India. His father had died many years before but he, the elder son, had been far away in the UK, and unable to carry out the needful funeral rites. He knew that in Rameshwaram he could perform *shraddh*, a sequence of rites that were believed to ease the transition of the parent's *atman* (soul) after death, and perhaps obviate the need for being born as a human yet again. I felt myself to be richly blessed, back once again at this hallowed spot, incorporated now in a Hindu genealogy, as well as being a student of the Hindu tradition. What overwhelmed me was the sense of perfect harmony between the natural setting (ocean, sand) and the religious ritual repeated through so many centuries, and between human activity and the animals and birds present who were intrinsic to the process.

As the poem relates, we arrived in the lunar month of *kartika* (October–November), and on the day of the full moon, which Hindus regard as especially auspicious. The poem refers to one of the priests (known as *panda*) who are available to cater for Hindus from different parts of India. Ours spoke Hindi, and specialised in Punjabi and other North Indian clients like my husband. The *gopuram* is the impressively sculpted, pylon-shaped gateway to the temple enclosure. The 'ancient sage' is the South Indian exponent of non-dualism, Shankara, who in the ninth century C.E. designated Rameshwaram as one of the Char Dham, four cardinal pilgrimage destinations for Hindus. The 'Brahmin thread', worn diagonally across the chest, is the *janeu*, the thread with which many high-caste males are ritually invested and which many only subsequently wear for their parents' funeral rites. The 'doughy balls' are the *pinda*s, kneaded on the priest's instruction as part of the required proceedings. 'Enwombed', recalling 'entombed', alludes to the temple's heart – in Hindu terminology its *garbagriha* or 'womb-house'. I used 'myriad' without apology to the denouncers of cliché: 'Shraddh' is, as I say, probably still a work in progress.

Coventry has been my home for nearly all my adult life. A new notice on the west door of the cathedral stirred me to write 'This entrance …'. A man's singing in Broadgate was the starting point for 'Buying Easter Cards'. Verses one and two of 'Waiting' result from time spent at Coventry bus stops and in Coventry hospital waiting rooms and led me to recall the bed-side waiting evoked in verse three. In 'Midlands snowfall' the experience of snow in Coventry takes me back to north India (as well as to my English childhood), as snow-covered roofs, resplendent at sunrise, transported me to one dawn in the 1970s when I had climbed to a local hilltop early enough to see the sun's first rays kindle the Himalayan peaks above Naini Tal. One of these, the highest at some 25,600 feet, and so the highest mountain completely in India, is Nanda Devi (literally bliss-giving Goddess), 75 miles away from Naini Tal in the Garhwal Himalaya.

My early immersion in the classics continues to influence what I write, by providing images and connecting with more contemporary concerns, as in 'Triodia' and 'Future signs'. The poem 'Future signs' alludes to ancient Roman practices of augury – foretelling the future by observing the direction in which birds flew or noting peculiarities in the entrails of sacrificial animals – and was the outcome of a week in which a scan in hospital more or less coincided with reading an article by Gill Westcott in UK Quakers' weekly publication, *The Friend*, about the world's loss if polar bears become extinct as global consumption escalates and the Arctic ice melts (2005: 17).

The subject of my final four poems is poetic creation. As the mystery of the poetic process endlessly tantalises me, from time to time another poem takes shape. Perhaps 'But What is Poetry?' conveys something of the incantatory credentials of poetry. (R.S. Thomas's summary: 'Poetry / is a spell woven / by consonants and vowels / in the absence of logic' now comes to mind (2004). About 'In Quaker Meeting' I have said something above. 'Suggestions' is a reminder of the part that a poetry group can play. As for my final poem, after one of the Diviners' meetings I asked Rowan Williams, at that time Archbishop of Wales, when he found time to write poems, and his reply was 'In airports'. 'Poems' was a much later consequence of this exchange. I conclude these paragraphs on spirituality and poetry with the images of landing and take-off.

This is my day

This is my day – sifted sand
shifting grain by invisible grain.
This is my day – a seed
lightly sown in the earth.
This is my day – a bud
to unfold in the sun, a flame
to protect from the wind,
a flickering wick in my shrine.
This is my day – a bowl
to be emptied or filled, a cup
to be proffered or drained.
This is my day – a page
to be written or read, a race
to be witnessed or run, a gem
to be cherished and polished
and given away.
This is your day.

Prayer

God make me gentle
Where the world is hard for living,
And where the world is harsh,
God make me kind for loving.

Examination question

'Hold us in the hollow of your hand:
Bless us with the radiance of your gaze;
Guide us, help us, succour and support;
Bring us safely to the promised land.'

Does human tendency to anthropomorphise
initiate, inhibit or distort
theology? Discuss – while life allows –
but do not try too hard to understand.

Healing

'Healing means you may write
no more poems', she says.
Are poems diagnoses or symptoms
of malfunction, malaise,
emotional imbalance?
Are poems pain, or at least
pain remembered?

Is verse cleansing discharge
or the abscess's swelling
and throbbing? Is verse welling
of tears? Is it weeping
and wailing, or the calm
after sobbing?
Are poems a day or two's scabbing
or permanent scarring?
Are they pain relief capsules
or laser lines searing,
cauterising and cutting?

Is healing anaesthetised
numbness or enhancement
of feeling? A stumbling and
dumbness
or songful cartwheeling
or silent at-oneness?
Poets aren't always sick or demented,
tormented or torn. Let my healing
bring hymns – hymns brimming with wholeness,
verse velvet as summer bees,
humming in sunlight,
homing through stillness.

Theodicy

Cancer and evil …
Cancer and evolution …
Even cancer and even odds …
But cancer and God – or gods…?

God contemplating and creating cancer?
God remonstrating, God berating cancer?
Is God inclement, impotent
Or just inconsequential?
Or is my cancer somehow Providential?

Thinking, searching, railing bring no answers.
Faith may console the faithful
Who take fewer chances
With punitive afterlife, but cancer's

Only answer comes to me in people's
Deep-down love and help and hope,
Their hanging on, their phone calls lasting hours,
Their prayers and smiles and messages
On cards and great bouquets of flowers,

And in the dawning sense that I can cope
With more than I had thought,
Being not alone, but caught
In unbreaking webs of gossamer support.

And when fear clings and haunts
And unintended words, more cruel than taunts,
Make optimism pale and every creed seem fantasy,
Another card or call, a country walk,
A trip to town or comfortable talk
Brings reassurance beyond any tried theodicy.

And I can call this God,
Or not, but must not set at nought
The transformation that this cancer's wrought.

The person you are calling...

Imagine just how many calls they must receive –
you would have thought they'd have an answer-phone
to play a pre-recorded tape.
Instead, just silence – seashell hush or, worse,
some indecipherable tones and bleeps.
If I go to their door it's much the same.
no-one appears, regardless of how long or loud
I ring the bell. Still no-one comes,
although I sometimes sense a warmth inside,
and think that I detect a curtain has been moved.
The road? No name, no numbers. Sometimes, undeterred,
I drop a letter in the post, in case,
though unaddressed, it finds its way – like children's
Christmas mail to Santa Claus in Lapland.
More frequently, I come and push my message
through the door. My decorated, perfumed envelopes,
elaborately inscribed, draw no response. Just once
I pressed a scribbled plea between the bricks.
and once I painted 'HELP ME!' and my name
in mirror writing over curtained panes.
They never came. 'They?' I do not know
if 'they' are one or many, he or she,
or if they've moved away. Callers I have met
have argued all these possibilities.
Some reason with each other, 'Look how beautiful
the garden is (or was). There must be somebody
who laid out flower beds and lawns, and someone
must be mowing, weeding, raking leaves', while others
find it overgrown, but have not seen a sale board.
Some say they come because their parents
told them to: 'Whoever does not come will face disaster.'
Persistent curiosity brings me, and memories –
ethereal music, once heard indistinctly,
through a keyhole.

Earthling Religion

Outside they worship birds.
They wheel their strapped-up young ones
to the edge of lakes,
then fill their fists with bread,
and help them sprinkle crumbs
among the outstretched necks.

Indoors they meditate
alone before a screen or, grouped
attentively, focusing as an image flits
and voices rise and fall.

Sometimes they build great metal birds.
They file inside to fly above the cloud,
then plunge back to their planet home.
One day I peered inside a swooping great bird's
hundred eyes and saw them
strapped inside, each one at prayer
as if for life.

Glastonbury (visited by the British Association for the Study of Religions)

We were no New Age travellers,
Pagans, pilgrims, Christians on retreat
Or on the march, but academics
Visiting the field. So there, where ley lines meet
And Joseph walked and scholars theorise,
We left the bus and went our several ways
To ruined abbey, bookshops and the Tor –
Tourists now, happy, eager to explore,
But still constrained to analyse, impress,
And never free to risk not seeming wise
Or smart. And there was I, unable to express
Or comprehend the Torward pull, the purging
And the peace. Inwardly changed and mute,
Tranquil, ecstatic, free, I caught the bus and sat
And heard myself attempt to joke and chat.

In Smethwick Rolfe Street

Remembering Adlestrop I will be bold
and write of Smethwick Rolfe Street
that October Sunday when the clocks went back.
The bright low sun made paper silhouettes
of sturdy trees. Sycamore leaves – golden,
yellow, lime – spun, pirouetting, trackwards
and a silver squirrel leapt, lightfoot
along a gantry. Wind-in-tree sounds
softly washed the track.

A name like Dhillon, Dhanjal, Dhaliwal,
Nagra – not Nesbitt – would license me
to pun in Punglish,[16] Smethwick's mother-tongue.
Punjabi metaphors drift from the gurdwara[17]
across the carriageway: hunger for langar,[18]
seva's[19] fulsome flavour, and a sangat (congregation)
washed by shimmering tides of hymns
(the kirtan)[20] curtaining them from England –
traffic, graffiti, and a railway station
fleetingly wondrous as a woodland shrine.

---

[16]   The spoken mix of Punjabi and English.

[17]   The Sikh place of worship.

[18]   Langar (rhymes with 'hunger'): the free, ample, vegetarian spread shared with all.

[19]   Seva (rhymes with 'flavour'): voluntary service such as providing, preparing and serving langar.

[20]   Kirtan (keyer-ton): singing of hymns, accompanied by tabla and harmonium.

Elephanta

'We Hindus do not worship broken images',
explains the guide in Elephanta's pillared cave.
Chiselled from living rock, Shiva – long limbless –
dance your cosmic dance, subject for tourist snaps
and serious study, but not for worship.

In me, perplexed post-Protestant,
last of a line that loved a broken Lord
and shared fragmented bread,
wonder still wells afresh from broken stone.

With neither priest nor prayers
my worship springs, cleanses and heals
in roofless shrines and desecrated, awesome caves.

Shraddh

'A good day – Kartika – full moon.'
A temple guide, hopeful of custom,
Greets us by the train, hears us explain
That we have come for Shraddh, come to perform
The rites that free the soul of the deceased
From more rebirths. He will, he says, ensure
That all is done aright.

Dwarfed by the temple's towering gopuram –
Tapering stone, alive with sculpted forms –
Pilgrims and vendors, beggars, cattle, crows
Are one with sea and sky,
One with the ancient sage's certainty
That all are one.

On the beach we sit, the priest
Banded with ashen marks, recites in Sanskrit,
Asking the names of the deceased. He is alert, prepared
With all we need – bananas, garlands, milk,
Coconut, flour, dried grasses
And umbrella, tucked away in case it rains.

Raucous crows, eager attentive goat, mild watchful cow
And you, hung with a Brahmin thread,
Naming your father, mother, kin,
Across the generations. Bidden by the priest
You knead the milk and flour to doughy balls.
A crow snaps one, the cow receives the rest.
The waves accept the garlands.
Obediently we give bananas to a cow along the way
Towards the temple, where the guide
Draws water from each sacred well,
Drenches you, guides us through
Pillared avenues to shadowed shrines
Arched by the steady glow of myriad flames,
Arch beyond arch.

Multi-dimensional infinity enwombed,
Space, time, present, past,
Life, death, all one
This fulsome, moonlit night
Of Kartika.

Midlands snow

Walking new snowfall, not yet packed
on hardened ice that footfall nearly cracks,
the word I hear is your word 'thwock'.
Thwocking (with concrete, tarmac, grass
now memories), I'm back with sledges,
snowmen, snowballs, when the world was
black and white. At eight a.m. today
ranges of recent roofs glow pearl and pink.
My legs recall their climb in Naini Tal
to watch as Nanda Devi came alight.
I watch the TV weather with suspense:
will snowflakes on the map reach Birmingham?
Excitement topples more pragmatic fear,
and snow, like rainbows and elusive scents,
connects and quickens, and then goes.

This entrance...

'This entrance is for worship, prayer and disability only'[21]

If what you want to do is look around
you need a ticket
at a different door.

Prayer, worship, disability are free.
Acknowledgment of need
will gain admission.

Be careful not to marvel at mosaic,
to stare at sculpture or stained glass
or organ pipes. Beware of looking
interested. Enthusiasm
should not be voiced.

Better to buy a ticket,
distance myself from disability,
attend to history and artistry.
But I can't guarantee
I will not pray.

---

[21]   Notice on West Door of Coventry cathedral in 2012.

Buying Easter cards

Daffodils mostly,
and in the cathedral shop
crosses and texts,
a Gothic arch or spire,
a tasteful altar and a
'May the blessing of the Risen Lord …'

In Smiths and Devlins,
among daffodils and primroses
and chocolate eggs,
bunnies and chicks with yellow envelopes
all wish us 'Happy Easter!'

Days lengthen, clocks change,
trees blossom, white and pink,
and lambs and baby ducks
perk up the countryside.
It seems that Easter (goddess, Spring)
is being briefly happy.

And in the city square,
where the asylum seekers often sit,
a man sings loud
and indistinct
about a wooden cross
and someone dying for our sins –

tasteless as death row
or genocide –

as we buy Easter cards
that will not offend.

Daffodils mostly.

Waiting

Waiting, we plan our day,
fumble for change.
Events and voices running through our heads,
we scan the road.
We chat – 'Nice weather' or
'It looks like rain.'
Then 'Here it is, at last',
and we are on our way.

Waiting, we plan our day,
fidget a bit,
flick through a magazine we'd never buy.
We weigh each other up:
'Here for a check up', or
'I wonder how she looked when she was young.'
Then 'Eleanor Nesbitt, please'
and I am out, alone.

Waiting, we do not dare
to think ahead
without you. Planning is too cruel.
We castigate ourselves for planning,
for not planning, and we watch
for any tremor,
glimmer, rattle, rasp.
We hold your hands.
We tell each other you seem comfortable.
You are alone.
We wait and pray.

Triodia

A place where three roads meets,
Fateful for road-rage Oedipus
And his mother;
Fatal for his father,
Fruitful for Sophocles and Freud.

T junction? Intersection?
This place where three roads meet –
Don't three roads meet wherever
One road bifurcates?
And every bifurcation is a road.

One place, interstice,
Site for predicted patricide,
To be transcribed and staged
As tragedy, now tessellated
In a century's neuroses.

Places where three roads meet
Are now equipped with roundabouts and
Traffic lights and any deaths are
Tragically accidental.

Future signs[22]

After two thousand years
our futures lie
in entrails again.

Our liver scans,
our lung X-rays
inform our plans.

The flight of birds
now augurs not
our futures only,
but the Earth's.

Too late we note
the plight of polar bears
and dare not hope
they lie.

---

[22]   Previously published in Florance and Nesbitt (2011: 106).

But what is poetry?

Hymns? Prayers? Spells?
Only what must be said,
Clean as a whistle,
Resonant as bells,
Keen as a blade, words
Whittled down to bone;
Pennies new-minted
Pitched longingly down wells;
Wishes, entreaties, mantras
Calling down the moon;
Tomorrow's hieroglyphs
And runes, today a-hum
With lilting tunes; crystals
Imprisoned, quartz in stone.
Prise out your sonnets! Liberate
Your villanelles!

In Quaker Meeting

'Ministry is like writing poetry', she said and I agreed.
But now, in Meeting, heartbeat gathering speed,
Certain I have to stand and break unbroken
Bonding silence; then relieved at having spoken,
I think, 'Is this what happens when a poem comes unbidden,
Propelled, insistent upon being written?'

Silence and clean white paper are alike receptive.
The urgency, the imperative to write are as directive
As feeling called to stand. Do verse and ministry
Well up from deep below or beckon from beyond? A mystery.

Each brings a resolution. Each seeks to resonate
With kindred spirits, to communicate.
Each flows from isolation to communion,
A sacrament of heart and word in union.

Suggestions

It's good. That line especially's
to die for. The transferred epithet
('the wakeful nightie') just makes verse three.
What haunting images! And those half-rhymes
work well. But don't you feel
the title needs to change? And those four words
could go. Remember: 'Show, not tell!'
And here, I smell a cliché.
The metre? Fine … you didn't know
you'd written iambs? Perhaps because
that's how we often speak. Yes, now,
I'd wait for several days, and then
reread. I think you may decide
to cut the final line.

Poems

Poems, you once said, come to you
in airports. I see you unencumbered,
slipping fetters of farewells and fears;
side-stepping sudokus and duty-free;
blessed by that solitude that crowds allow:
alert for more than boardings
and delays.

Solid and sure, some taxi smoothly in,
spilling their metaphors across
your waiting page. Others are
disappearing wisps of white,
a distant glint, a thrum
as you embark.

References

Arnold, Matthew, 'Dover Beach' available at http://www.victorianweb.org/authors/arnold/writings/doverbeach.html Accessed 13 October 2012

Arweck, Elisabeth and Martin D. Stringer (eds), *Theorizing Faith: The Insider/Outsider Problem in the Study of Ritual* (Birmingham: University of Birmingham Press, 2002)

Askari, Hasan, Mauricio Garcia-Duran, Molly Kenyon and Jenny Litaba (eds), *Faith and Friendship: In Memory of David Bowen* (Bradford: Bradford College, 2002)

Bailey, R.V., *Marking Time* (Calstock: Peterloo Poets, 2004)

Bailey, R.V., *The Losing Game* (Edinburgh: Mariscat Press, 2010)

Bailey, R.V., *Credentials: New and Selected Poems* (South Pool: Oversteps Books Ltd, 2012)

Barrett Browning, Elizabeth, 'Aurora Leigh' in D.H.S. Nicholson and A.H.E. Lee (eds), *The Oxford Book of English Mystical Verse* (Oxford: Oxford University Press, 1917)

Blake, William, 'Auguries of Innocence' in J. Sampson (ed.), *The Poetical Works of William Blake* (Oxford: Oxford University Press, 1952)

Bowman, Marion, 'Understanding Glastonbury as a Site of Consumption' in Gordon Lynch, Jolyon Mitchell and Anna Strhan (eds), *Religion, Media and Culture: A Reader* (Abingdon: Routledge, 2011) 11–22

Bowra, C.M. (trans.), *The Odes of Pindar* (Harmondsworth: Penguin, 1969)

Britain Yearly Meeting of the Religious Society of Friends (Quakers) in Britain, *Quaker Faith and Practice: The Book of Discipline of the Yearly Meeting of the Religious Society of Friends (Quakers) in Britain* (London: Britain Yearly Meeting of the Religious Society of Friends (Quakers) in Britain, 2008, 4th edn)

Chandan, Amarjit, *Being Here* (London: The Many Press, 2005)

Cope, Wendy, *Serious Concerns* (London: Faber, 1992)

Dear, Anna (ed.), *Poetry as Pilgrimage* (unpublished collection, privately circulated 2012)

Durham, Geoffrey, *Being a Quaker: A Guide for Newcomers* (Quaker Quest, 2011)

Eck, Diana L., 'Dialogue and Method: Reconstructing the Study of Religions', in Kimberley C. Patton and Benjamin C. Ray (eds), *A Magic Still Dwells:*

Comparative Religion in The Postmodern Age (Berkeley and Los Angeles: University of California Press, 2000)

Eliot, T.S., *Collected Poems 1909–1962* (New York: Harcourt, Brace & World, 1963)

Fanthorpe, U.A., *New and Collected Poems* (London: Enitharmon Press, 2010)

Florance, Ian and Eleanor Nesbitt (eds), *Gemini Four*, (Henley-on-Thames: OnlyConnect, 2011)

Gardner, W.H. and N.H. MacKenzie (eds), *The Poems of Gerard Manley Hopkins* (London: Oxford University Press, 1970)

Gautier, Théophile, Émaux et Camées (Paris: Librairie Garnier Frères, 1872)

Geertz, Clifford, *The Interpretation of Cultures* (New York: Basic Books, 1973)

Gross, Philip, *The Water Table* (Tarset: Bloodaxe, 2009)

Gross, Philip, *Deep Field* (Tarset: Bloodaxe, 2011)

Guite, Malcolm, *Faith, Hope and Poetry: Theology and the Poetic Imagination* (Aldershot: Ashgate, 2010)

Heaney, Seamus and Ted Hughes (eds), *The Rattle Bag* (London: Faber & Faber, 1982)

Herbert, George 'Prayer', *The Poetical Works of George Herbert* (New York: D. Appleton and Co, 1857) 61–2

Hick, John, *The Fifth Dimension: An Exploration of the Spiritual World* (Oxford: Oneworld, 1999)

Hopkins, Gerard Manley, *Poetry and Prose*, ed. Walford Davies (London: Everyman, 1998)

Jackson, Robert and Eleanor Nesbitt, *Hindu Children in Britain* (Stoke on Trent: Trentham, 1993)

Krayer, Stevie, *Questioning the Comet* (Ceredigion: Gomer, 2004)

Latham, R.E. (trans.), *Lucretius On the Nature of the Universe* (Harmondsworth: Penguin, 1951)

Lewis, Gwyneth, 'How to Knit a Poem', *Poetry Review* (no date) available at http://www.poetrysociety.org.uk/lib/tmp/cmsfiles/File/review/Volume%20 97/971%20Lewis.pdf Accessed 20 September 2012

Nagra, Daljit, *Look, We Have Coming to Dover* (London: Faber and Faber, 2007)

Nesbitt, Eleanor, *Turn But a Stone* (Norwich: Hilton House, 1999)

Nesbitt, Eleanor, 'Quaker Ethnographers: A Reflexive Approach', in Elisabeth Arweck and Martin D. Stringer (eds), *Theorising Faith: The Insider/Outsider Problem in the Study of Ritual* (Birmingham, University of Birmingham Press: 2002) 133–54

Nesbitt, Eleanor, *Interfaith Pilgrims: Living Truth and Truthful Living* (London: Quaker Books, 2003)

Nesbitt, Eleanor, *Sikhism: A Very Short Introduction* (Oxford: Oxford University Press, 2005)

Nesbitt, Eleanor, 'But What Does Ethnography Have to Do with Me?' *Resource*, 23/3 (2006) 4–8

Nesbitt, Eleanor, 'Interrogating the Experience of Quaker Scholars in Hindu and Sikh Studies: Spiritual Journeying and Academic Engagement', *Quaker Studies*, 14/2 (2010) 134–58

Nesbitt, Eleanor and Gopinder Kaur, *Guru Nanak* (Calgary: Bayeux Arts, 1999)

Newey, Adam, review of Glyn Maxwell *On Poetry*, *Guardian Review*, 18, 14 July 2012 Available at http://www.guardian.co.uk/books/2012/jul/13/on-poetry-glyn-maxwell-review Accessed 26 April 2013

Page, D.L. (ed.), *Lyrica Graeca Selecta* (Oxford: Oxford University Press, 1968)

Piirto, Jane, 'The Question of Quality and Qualifications: Writing Inferior Poems as Qualitative Research', *International Journal of Qualitative Studies in Education*, 15/4 (2002) 431–45

Pullman, Philip, *The Good Man Jesus and the Scoundrel Christ* (London: Canongate, 2011)

Pym, Jim, *The Pure Principle: Quakers and Other Faith Traditions* (York: William Sessions, 2000)

Ricks, Christopher (ed.), *The Oxford Book of English Verse* (Oxford: Oxford University Press)

Riis, Ole and Linda Woodhead, *A Sociology of Religious Emotion* (Oxford: Oxford University Press, 2010)

Ruth, Sibyl, 'A Song of Jean', *Mslexia*, 28 (2008) 34. Available at http://www.mslexia.co.uk/magazine/newwriting/nwpoem1_38.php Accessed 20 July 2012

Schmidt, Michael (ed.), *The Harvill Book of Twentieth-Century Poetry in English* (London: The Harvill Press, 1999)

Schmidt-Leukel, Perry, *Transformation through Integration: How Inter-Faith Encounter Changes Christianity* (London: SCM Press, 2009)

Skeie, Geir, 'Plurality and Pluralism: A Challenge to Religious Education', *British Journal of Religious Education*, 17/2 (1995) 84–91

Tennyson, Alfred, 'In Memoriam' (no date) available at http://www.theotherpages. org/poems/books/tennyson/tennyson01.html Accessed 13 October 2012

Thomas, R.S., *Collected Later Poems: 1988–2000* (Tarset: Bloodaxe, 2004)

Thompson, Francis, 'The Kingdom of God' in D.H.S. Nicholson and A.H.E. Lee (eds), *The Oxford Book of English Mystical Verse* (Oxford: Oxford University Press, 1917)

Topping, Angela, 'How to Capture a Poem' in R. Longdell (ed.), *Troubles Swapped for Something Fresh, Manifestos and Unmanifestos* (Cambridge: Salt, 2009) available at http://sicttasd.tripod.com/angelatopping/ Accessed 20 September 2012

Westcott, Gill, 'Polar Bears and Canaries', *The Friend*, 163/51 (2005, 23&30 December) 17

Whittier, John Greenleaf, *The Works of Whittier, Volume I (of VII) Narrative and Legendary Poems* (2009) available at http://www.gutenberg.org/ files/9567/9567-h/9567-h.htm#link2H_4_0085 Accessed 26 April 2013

Wordsworth, William, 'Preface to Lyrical Ballads' (1800). Available at http:// www.bartleby.com/39/36.html Accessed 20 September 2012

Chapter 5

The Miracle of Poetry: Divine and Human Creativity

Gavin D'Costa

Walking the Dog for the First Time

It is autumn as I write. A dog walker told me this morning that she had seen a miracle. This kind of language is not usual in Bristol's early morning dog-walking fraternity. What had she seen: a lame dog pick up its bedding and walk? a blind dog leap into the air and catch a tennis ball? I urged her on with a quizzical look. She pointed at the trees that bank the tennis court in the middle of the park. In the space of two days the canopy had begun to change into russet reds, gentle greys, hazy yellows, and rusty browns. She had been away a few days and returned to see a different park. The bright autumn morning light celebrated this miracle, playing off the colours into patterns with the autumnal breeze. Yes, it was a miracle: leaves transformed. She used the word miracle colloquially, but perhaps with a real sense of one element of this curious word: seeing something familiar anew. T.S. Eliot had recognised that element of miracle in his poem 'Little Gidding' when he wrote how the end of our exploring is to arrive just where we started, 'And know the place for the first time' (Eliot, 1963: 222). This woman and I were seeing the same park we walk in every day 'for the first time'. And it was a joy. And it was good.

Anyone in England who has read Philip Larkin's 'Church Going' will probably have experienced the miracle of walking into an empty English village church and seeing it again through Larkin's haunting phrases, maybe for 'the first time' in his way (Larkin, 1990: 97–8). Something that is always there gets given shape and form through unfamiliar words: that musty scent and sound as we hear our own feet on the cobble stones, some of them covered in moss green coats, or even on the old graveyard flagstones in the church that mean we walk over the dead; that sense that people who come here, perhaps including ourselves, visit for all sorts of curious reasons; and because of some deeper instinct that this old church is a 'serious house on serious earth'. This primal ancestral quality of the building's history is also its power and enchantment. My own experience of 'good' poetry is that it takes me up, tumbles me round, and life is different after that encounter. Sometimes it is not clear how. But, I suspect, that is what makes me read, listen and try to write poetry. It is a journey into an 'undiscover'd country, from whose bourn No traveller returns' unchanged, including the writer perhaps (Shakespeare, 1891).

The Miracle of Poetry

I don't want to be bracketed as a religious nutcase talking about poetry as miracle, but I do want to make a serious claim that has fuelled my love of poetry, whether reading, hearing or writing it. The claim is simple: if it makes you see differently, then it is miraculous. Wikipedia is quite helpful here. Substitute the word 'poet' for the word 'miracle worker' as you read. It says of a miracle:

> A miracle is an event attributed to divine intervention. Alternatively, it may be an event attributed to a miracle worker, saint, or religious leader. A miracle is sometimes thought of as a perceptible interruption of the laws of nature. Others suggest that God may work *with* the laws of nature to perform what people see as miracles. Theologians say that, with divine providence, God regularly works through created nature yet is free to work without, above, or against it as well. (http://en.wikipedia.org/wiki/Miracle – all sites checked December 2012)

I would not like to substitute poet for 'saint or religious leader', but the visionary element of poetry does have an important relation with the role of a preacher. William Blake's poems are fiery sermons that leave me unsettled. Sadly, not enough sermons achieve that. What I like about the definition is that it keeps a tension present and unresolved: miracles might not be seeing Clark Kent, aka Superman, whizz across the sky in black leggings and red cape; they may not be like seeing a blind dog healed and leap into the air and catch a ball. A miracle might be like seeing the transformation in the blind dog's owner to cope with a blind dog and to help her dog deal with its doggy life. A miracle might be like suddenly feeling sympathy and understanding for a person we have normally thought to be weak and feckless. And it might be seeing a leaf anew and marvelling at its beauty. I do not want to secularise miracles nor divinise poetry. What I do want to do is stay with the boundary lines between these two zones, that become so porous, and in that process so interesting. There is an intriguing Hindu tale to indicate the nature of 'insight', *darshan*, that is attributed to the great Hindu sage Shankara. A man walks along the road towards a well and sees a snake lying in the dust across his path. He is worried. He finds a stick so that he might push the snake off the road. But as he gets near he suddenly realises, has the insight, that the snake is not a snake at all, but a rope. He might have been told by a friend that this was not a snake, but a rope. But whichever version we hear, it requires in the man an act of insight, realisation, that will change his perception and practices. The rope was always there – it had not changed. He had. He is now able to see it as a rope: for what it truly is. This word *darshan* is sometimes used as synonymous for 'revelation', although the nature of the 'given' in revelation may have a different historical dimension in Jewish and Christian thought than it does in Indian thought. They should not be easily conflated.

I want to claim for poetry something more than a kind of epistemological shift, more than just a different way of seeing something. I want to claim that if the seeing differently is successful, there is, to use the jargon, an ontological shift as well. One actually encounters a new and perhaps different reality because of the shift in insight. Poetry can damage your health! It has the power to take you to different worlds – and the line between truth and falsity in so-called fictitious worlds is notoriously difficult to locate.

Different Seeing and Different Worlds

It might help if I say a little about my own life path in terms of characterising poetry in this way, as miracle. I was born into a devout Roman Catholic family. I was born into hybridity, which I took to be the norm, and have slowly discovered that it is indeed the norm. Everything is made up of many things and multiple identities. I'm not a thorough postmodern, as something seems to hold together these multiple and fluid identities. That something may be bigger than the individual. My parents were Indians of the Empire, shipped out to work in the colonies, in Kenya, East Africa. In Nairobi, I was raised in an area where the sky lit up at Diwali, where the Muslim kids were subdued during Ramadan, except after nightfall, and where we Christians had Father Christmas figures adorning houses that had no chimneys. Religion was part of the furniture and history, the cosmos, and all ritual life received multiple narrations that co-existed in a friendly and peaceable manner. The main thing was that the neighbours were nice, and from my child's point of view, shared sweets at major festivals. I relished Diwali. It was from religion that I imbibed poetry, not because my parents belonged to an elite cultural group who indulged in poetry readings *per se*, but rather because we used to go to Mass every Sunday and my parents said the rosary every night.

The Mass at Nairobi Cathedral, before the changes of Vatican II had been rung in, was in Latin. I recall my childish wonder at a ceremony that linguistically 'meant' so little (I did not know Latin), but sounded so musical and magical. It was accompanied by scented wreaths of smoky incense and bells that could have driven fire engines off the road. The priest used to dress up like no one I'd ever seen, even Superman, and his gold and purple robes would shine in the spotlight that focused on the altar. When he held the host up I knew I was witnessing a miracle: the transformation of normal materials from the earth into the site of God's visitation to us. The Eucharist has always filled me with awe, not least because we eventually consume it so that it makes up our own bodies. Even as a child I marvelled that this joyful celebration all centred round the torture and death of a human person. It didn't make sense at all, but it seemed very right: that God was here, with us, in joy and in suffering and pain. I knew both. The site of the sacred was the site of ritual chanting, musical meditation, and of course, sometimes utter boredom and bewilderment. This event in the midst of normal-day life was, my mum told me, supposed to transform my normal life. I had to leave the church and be Jesus to others. I discovered that I was better at seeing how Jesus was coming to me in others. The psalms were also sung, sometimes in parts, and my sister and I droned on, pretending to know what we were singing, but loving the possibility that our droning chimed in with the shape of the chant. Here was poetry sung together, communally enacted, and supposedly life transforming. I think this childhood experience marked me. It is why I began to know, even before thinking about it, that poetry has miraculous qualities.

The rosary had the same power. Ask any Buddhist or Muslim who uses prayer beads. My parents would say and repeat the prayers (Our Father, Glory be, Hail Mary, and the litany of saints – where our family favourites were named singly – Saints Teresa, Rock, Elizabeth, Ignatius, and so on, and then we chanted 'pray for us' after each saint's name). One of our cousins, a highly expert rosary-sayer, had perfected the ability to say the whole rosary in under seven minutes due to the speed of his prayer. Listening to him made my sister and me giggle. We couldn't giggle during his praying, only after. Although he spoke in English, it might as well have been Latin, given his amazing speed and focus. Whatever it sounded like (and it was not always exactly the same) we knew what was being said, and the music of the words whizzing by was lovely. The rosary, for all its demands on a young child, has the comfort of being prayed as a family: my mum, dad, sister and I would travel down the tracks together. It has an association of security, being held in the love and protection of my human family and through this, the divine family. The Father, Son and the Holy Spirit, were present, but also in a very comforting manner we were being held and supported by Mary and all the saints (I especially liked Philomena, Felicity, and Perpetua). It felt like half of heaven was here making life on earth seem bearable or good. Often enough, I just fell asleep in the chanting or wanted to lie half-asleep being washed by this holy wave of musical sound. It taught me something about musical words: they can bore, send you to sleep, or they can transform the world.

In childhood, lots of other poetry was happening: children's rhymes at school and the thrill of creating our own naughty rhymes or ones that would poke fun at a teacher; the Kikkiku songs of my African 'aiya' (maid or nanny) as she cooked her food on an open fire; and the poetry of my dad's stories. He was a great story teller and purveyor of jokes. Late at night, especially when we had relatives or friends visiting, he would tell ghost stories. They were dramatic: long pauses that had me hiding in my mother's coat, covering my head, terrified of the event to be related; and critical moments when someone might make a joke just to relieve the tension and we'd all hoot with laughter – knowing it would be short-lived. All of these experiences changed us together. They were communal stories creating a communal bond. They were done for the fun, but they also made us one. Where there had been something before, now there was more, with the 'something' still intact. Reflecting on this, I'm struck at how individualistic and solitary is my general experience of poetry today, where I read in silent attention alone at night, or in the train, or in the bath. Or, just sometimes, with my poetry group or my dear wife: my two communal contexts of reading and listening. But there is something that connects all these experiences together: words changing the feel of reality, enacting a kind of miracle in perception, engendering a new conception.

Flight into England

Language is of course far more complex and highly ambivalent. I have focused on just one aspect, but this aspect has continued to haunt me as I grew up. When I came to England just before Idi Amin's escaping Ugandan Asians filed up at Heathrow after Jomo Kenyatta's Kenyan Asians had done earlier, I learnt two things about poetry. The first was that I knew and continue to know only elements of the western Latin Christian tradition. That is a shameful reality. I've read the *Upanishads* in translation and heard the *Gita* sung in Sanskrit on the banks of the Ganges and in the temples of Birmingham, but these were not my languages or my poetic traditions, even though I am Indian. There is some irony in the possibility that English Eleanor in our poetry group is more Indian than Indian Gavin. Hybridity has that effect. The second was that I realised that poetry in Bedford, where we settled and I was educated up until 18, was the preserve of the effete and the elite. The rugger-buggers had their street form of poetry – bawdy verse; and the poets of my school, including me, most of whom were librarians, shared their works on the library notice board and even had a couple of public recitals. We would sometimes comment on a poem to its author, but we were an aesthetic community that prized ourselves for our good taste and forms of decorum. One of our number got published and went on to Oxford to read English. This confirmed our self-image. The social register of poetry had changed dramatically from my childhood, but then so had everything else. I had come to a new society and was initially greeted by mild and ignorant racism as well as some kind and big-hearted boys from my school. I realised that to 'succeed' and to be accepted, at least in my view of things then, I had to be 'white'. I was slowly becoming a deeply Anglicised Kenyan Asian (that is the polite designation). My Christian roots meant there was no firewall to call me back 'home', as I imagine might be the case with a Hindu or

Sikh who wants to resist total Anglicisation. All the more so, as my Christianity was inherited from the Portuguese. Things are complicated even in India as the ancient Mar Thoma Christians still have their liturgy in Syriac, in part preserving their 'identity' and their claimed lineage from the Apostle Thomas. English was my first language and I had grown up with some American TV that was shown in Nairobi after its 'best by' date had expired in the United States. Writing poetry identified me with the aesthetes and cultural elites and I was near top of my class in English literature. It is at some level what I wanted. But I also just wanted to write, for fun, for its own sake. And I loved English literature because it constantly opened up new worlds and I was intoxicated with the beauty of language. I was experimenting with poetic voices and at the same time my own cultural identity was equally fluid. But amidst these experiments I can identify two themes that have continued in my poetry.

The first is the voice of someone who observes and is slightly outside the frame. Even with my attempt to assimilate to the cultural elites I still knew that I was not one of them: I was not white. My hybridity meant that there was no convenient 'home', no easy frame of belonging, but a sense of critical distance which sometimes struggled with 'alienation'. I don't say this with great strength of feeling as I encountered very little racism as I mounted the steps of academic achievement. The Catholic culture in Bedford was closely tied up with the large Irish community, and my school was not Catholic, but secular with the sprinkling of Anglican state religion characteristic of so many schools from the 1970s. I think that having polio as a child and a number of operations also contributed to my feeling an 'outsider', or at least at the margins, watching others with attention (and sometimes envy). I wrote poems that looked on at society, often in a critical and, so I imagined, prophetic, manner. Bob Dylan was one of my heroes for he seemed to question angrily the conventions of his society. This leads to my second early voice.

The second voice is a preoccupation with God and the childish (and properly so?) desire to 'belong' to God, to come to know and participate in the divine life through the ordinary. As a teenager I had a vision of two paths ahead of me: to become a Jesuit priest and teach theology at a university; or to get married and teach theology at a university. I cannot explain the teaching theology bit as I'd never formally studied theology and I loved English literature. But my minor readings in Aquinas and Aristotle in my early teens made me realise that theology was the place I would call 'home'. I was drawn by the clarity and desire to grasp complexity. There was a beauty in the simplicity of Aquinas and Aristotle: neither wasted a word. They had an asceticism of language through which they tried to attain a comprehensive purity of vision. Aquinas was always drawn by the fact that he would not and could not achieve this comprehensive vision, pushed to his knees by the mystery of God that enveloped his towering mind. The tensions resolved: I went on to study English and Theology at Birmingham University, a wonderful marriage of my two great intellectual loves. I also went on to Birmingham to meet my eventual wife, Beryl, and discovered that my vocation to the Jesuits had less pull than my vocation to being carnally embodied. But the common denominator in both of the two paths was being slowly achieved: I would become a theology lecturer.

Educating the Heart

When studying English at university, I discovered the poetry of Gerard Manley Hopkins through Beryl and the revelation in his work that God was just as present in the leaves of autumn as anywhere else: 'The world is charged with the grandeur of God' (Hopkins, 1967: 66). While Hopkins lived in the same empirical world as Larkin, he saw that world differently through his Jesuit spiritual eyes. In reading his poetry, I connected to the sacramentality of my earlier childhood: things, just the normal, mediate the divine. One sees more than sticks and stones and bones when one stumbles upon the site of the sacred. The relics of the true cross, the stones from *Scala Sancta*, and the bones of so many saints had done their work. If I could not see the sacred in these ruins and inanimate objects, I would not see it at all.

Seeing is too visual a metaphor. Language is always performative. Take the phrase: 'sit down' or 'look at those autumn leaves'. These are rather obvious, but there is a performative element in Larkin and Hopkins: both invite you to look at and act in the world in a particular manner. They do not force you to, but their 'force' is rhetorically achieved. One may be a cheerful optimist, but T.S. Eliot's 'The Hollow Men' shocked me into seeing western culture's barbarism and cliché-ridden communication. This was called into question before my very eyes and ears as I descended into the poem. And Eliot demands the tongue and eyes and mind and the will be reshaped to restore this fallen culture, where in his Augustinian view of humans, they are: 'Leaning together / Headpiece filled with straw' (Eliot, 1963: 89). I was attracted by Eliot's poetic-prophet role (remember the Wiki definition above). However, I knew from William Carlos Williams, especially in his 'The Red Wheelbarrow' that overly ideological or didactic poetry might crush the particular in front of us, when 'so much depends' on looking as truthfully, and therefore self-critically, as possible at something like a 'red wheelbarrow' (Williams, 1976: 57). There is a subtle relationship between the given and our construal of it. It is a question of the etiquette of truth: that we do not somehow damage the particularity of what we see by fitting it forcefully into a pre-shaped narrative; and yet our seeing is always in some form of narrative. My own poetry, as an undergraduate, continued with the two themes above, but now began to attend to romantic love and erotic desire, the profane Jesuit in me, as well as social events and their complexity – the outsider/insider observer. And both related to a desire to see God.

At the end of my undergraduate studies I knew that theology and English literature were doing something similar: they were arranging the world into a narrative, inviting the viewer/reader/practitioner to be changed and transformed through the process. They achieved their goals through different rhetorical strategies and there was a strong tension in me between the love of a story-shaped world (novels, the bible, Thomas à Kempis) and a systematic philosophically shaped world-view (Aristotle, Aquinas, and the great modern giants Karl Barth, who returned to narrative, and Karl Rahner, who idolised German Romantic philosophy). I was torn: I did not want to give up English nor reject Theology. I loved English, but I loved and communally practised theology. The latter won. Off I went to Cambridge University to do a doctorate in the Divinity Faculty. I sort of knew I could continue to write poetry even if I did not continue to formally study literature.

Doctoring the Mind

I chose to study an analytical philosopher theologian, John Hick, for my doctorate. With no disrespect to John at all, who was an inspiring and challenging person and writer, that was a slight nail in the coffin to my poetic sensibilities (only for a little while). Analytical philosophy at the time was keen on meaning and intelligibility and conceptual rigour – and that is what I loved about it. It also meant that with a particular strain of it in the 1980s, it was inimical to 'God', who could not be verified or falsified, and thus was no different from a fantasy character that lived in an invisible green shed at the bottom of the garden. Hick, with skill and analytical ability, tried to refute the notion that God was meaningless. He did this by staying on the terrain of the critics, rather than refusing to play God-ball on this turf. In this move he tacitly accepted that empirical verification was a good criterion for all meanings. This was a serious tactical mistake. By walking along this road for myself, I began to enter into a dark night of the soul, or more prosaically, I lost my faith. The world seemed utterly ordinary and the sacred had withdrawn into fantasy, rather than shining through ordinary 'dappled things' (Hopkins, 1967: 69). I didn't write too much during this period – which retrospectively is perhaps indicative of something: that poetry was a way of trying to communicate some participation in the divine life. This was an arid two years, but important in the process of growing up and seeing things, yet again, quite differently. It was also vitally important to be able to see the world from a different perspective and realise the compelling sensibility of structuring visions. If one was an agnostic, one usually had good, even if not entirely examined, reasons for being agnostic. 'Reason' here may denote a range of things: upbringing, prejudices, conceptual presuppositions, and so on. Life revealed itself in its wonderful complexity.

What changed me into a believer again? An action poem of sorts. It was Sanskrit chanting, temple bells, and incense smells in a small rural village in South India by the banks of the Kaveri River. I was doing research in India (I had decided to compare Hick with the Hindu philosopher Sarvapelli Radhakrishnan. I was living at Bede Griffiths's ashram, Shantivanam. I loved the liturgy: chanting Indian *bhajans* (devotional songs), having long silences before the consecrated Eucharist, and breathing/chanting the sacred syllable 'om' as a mantra of communion with the divine life. It was all a bit 1960s and alternative. But it was also utterly real and powerful. I realised that the life of faith would die if it relied on the head and that I was choked and strangled by not returning to the fountains and streams that were present in the church, primarily in its liturgy and its sometimes outrageous saints and in some of its remarkable theologians. The power of the poetic liturgy made me see anew and realise that I was at the place I had started out, seeing it freshly for the first time, but with a renewed heart and sense of creativity. Theology had made me run ahead with my mind whereas my emotions and imagination had been undereducated and unemployed. I saw that the ancient liturgy, over-familiar and therefore stale, had a life-giving power by making me look outside of myself towards a world of creativity, healing power, and new beginnings. God never accepted defeat but 'achieved' this miraculously through weakness, not technological or state power, through the cross. I started writing again and my theology became more grounded. I could imagine that being a theology lecturer was indeed the *telos* of my academic life rather than just the goal of a childhood ambition. Or both.

None of the poems I have chosen come from the period I have narrated. The life path since then has been the source of the poems chosen and I will speak about them in the final section of this chapter.

Real Presence

I want to return to the theme of poetry as miracle. This is not because the theology lecturer in me cannot be repressed but because I think this claim is so central to what I do as a poet. I should say immediately that when I write poetry, I have no lofty thoughts in my head such as: 'let me try and produce a miracle'. There is something right in William Wordsworth's claim that poetry is generated by the 'spontaneous overflow of powerful emotions recollected in tranquillity' (Wordsworth, 1800: 24). The tranquillity has usually been in the shape of a bus, plane or train travelling on work matters. In fact some of the poems are generated from and about this travel. The tranquillity has had to battle with mobile phones and announcements of increasing delays because of a signal failure in the Reading or Birmingham area. It is a tranquillity snatched when too exhausted or distracted to read and too overcome by some powerful emotion to do other than write. If my wife had been on the train, I would have probably talked to her instead about these events. Some poems come out of a loneliness.

After writing it I usually labour at the poem and rework it trying to find precisely that 'powerful emotion', trying to find the right shape for what I want to say and what needs to be said. It is in this process that the 'givenness' of the 'powerful emotion' becomes very significant as it demands a type of shape to say

it and perhaps the 'success' of a poem is whether the shape speaks when heard.
I do not mean anything esoteric here. Consider Hamlet's ode: 'Oh, that this too,
too sullied flesh would melt / Thaw, and resolve itself into a dew'. What makes
those lines so poignant is precisely the form: it captures the desire possibly to
'cease upon the midnight ', for Shakespeare rather than Keats, precisely because
of the pain Hamlet is experiencing (Keats, 1970: 529). Keats is trying to capture
something in the thought of dying and Hamlet seeks to lose something by the act
of dying. It expresses that sense of melting despair. Keats' desire for extinction
is utterly different. My poem will then be tried out on various kind and critical
listeners: the Diviners and my wife mainly, but there are others who have been
generous and critical. I will then chip away at the poem, sometimes returning to
them after many years, but on rereading they still seem unsatisfactory. Reading
them aloud is also helpful in hearing them and sensing where they might change.
They are curious birthlings which have their own autonomy when read, while also
having a genealogy tied up in their writing. The genealogy should be shed so that
they can be read without narratives other than their own. But their own narrative
shape always points to something other than the direct object of their concern.
There is always, as George Steiner puts it, a 'real presence' invoked by a work of
art (Steiner, 1989). Steiner thoughtfully speaks of a transcendence invoked by the
very creation of another world within the work of art. To me that transcendence
has a name. While the name by definition cannot capture the transcendence, the
name is the right shape and form for that transcendence. It is the name that takes
up each element that constitutes the finite and makes it the point of intersection
with the infinite: it is the miracle of the incarnation, a word that seems to be the
epiphany of the metaphors of transcendence and immanence.

The Genesis of Poetry

Let me try and put more shape to this claim. Poetry is a miracle just as being alive
is like a miracle. Why existence at all, rather than nothing? This is the primal
poetic act found in the book of Genesis. I think we keep company with God in
the act of writing. How? Because, God suggests, according to the narrator, that
speaking could be a miracle of divine participation as well as human communion.

Genesis 1 opens with the act of creation, where God speaks, indeed poetically chants the world into being:

> In the beginning God created heaven and earth. Now the earth was a formless void, there was darkness over the deep, with a divine wind sweeping over the waters. God said, 'Let there be light,' and there was light. God saw that light was good, and God divided light from darkness. God called light 'day' and darkness he called 'night'. Evening came and morning came: the first day. (http://www.catholic.org/bible/book.php; as with all biblical quotes, although when appropriate equally gendered).

'Let there be ...' or 'Let ...' starts each birthing push. And it is interesting that God uses language prior to the actual structures, shapes and forms emerging. When God said 'Let there be light' could anyone know what this would be? And then that which was light is called 'Day', it is given a name which is not 'night', not the 'darkness'. And 'day' only takes its force and significance from 'night', and also from its not being 'water' or the 'great sea monsters' or the other names. Why God had to use language is a total mystery as there is no one except God to speak to in the narrative. Was God talking to Himself? There is an interesting clue in verse 26: 'God said, "Let us make the human in our own image, in the likeness of ourselves [bɔ·ṣal·mê·nū; נַעֲשֶׂה בְּצַלְמֵנוּ – the Hebrew is plural; so God could have been talking to Himself] and let the human be masters of the fish of the sea, the birds of heaven, the cattle, all the wild animals and all the creatures that creep along the ground." So God created man in his *own* image, in the image of God created He him; male and female created She them ...' So if we are created in the image of God and God is an inveterate language user, and it is a human writer who writes this account of divine creation, we can see that language is the precondition for form and meaning, pleasure and joy, and communication, both between the divine and the human and between human persons.

There are two other features that help give us a deeper glimpse into divine creativity. We can say that material creation is actually birthed in speech, out of nothing, given shape by words, and that this creation was 'good'. Indeed, at every stage of this outrageous creativity, there is a moment of passivity, a standing back and taking it all in, perhaps in silent wonder: 'And God saw that it was good'.

Note that God does not speak this recognition, although God seems to be full
of musical chatter otherwise. God responds to the beauty of creation in silence.
It is in the space between words and without words that something remarkable
happens: awe. It is the writer's words that create the noise of communicating this
silence. And note further, at the end of the creation narrative, it is only after the
human chatterboxes are created that God gets carried away in wonder: 'And God
saw everything that She had made, and behold, it was *very* good.' Not just good,
but 'very good'. The whole in its interrelationship is greater than the parts. The act
of creation is 'very good', perhaps especially when it mirrors this divine creativity.

The other feature to note is that in the second act of creation narrated in
Genesis 2: 4–24 the naming function is handed over to the human being. It is quite
a different story for what is really remarkable in the first account: creation out of
divine speech acts (first account) is now transferred to the human speech acts,
humans made in God's image. It is the 'human' who names creation, a creation
which is paraded in front of the human person, and these names are taken seriously
by God.

> So from the soil the Lord God fashioned all the wild animals and all the birds
> of heaven. These he brought to the man to see what he would call them; each
> one was to bear the name the man would give it. The man gave names to all the
> cattle, all the birds of heaven and all the wild animals. But no helper suitable for
> the man was found for him.

Did he need a helper to find more names? No, the helper is actually required for
friendship, for love, and to literally continue the process of creation.

Language, Love and Lack

Following this story of language would take us through so many biblical stories,
too many to recount now. But the medley would include the way language finally
collapses in the tower of Babel (Genesis 11: 1–9), the end result of the misuse
of language: not for loving communication and creation, but for attaining our
own goals in an utterly singular manner – through driving ambition, through

creating a false but manageable world because it is not open to love, vulnerability and weakness? There are myriad ways of kidding ourselves that we are doing God's will when actually we are simply settling into old habits of achievement, attainment, 'service' and so on. The tower of language collapses and the dust really does not settle. It is not until Pentecost (Acts 2) that the Babel of language that causes confusion and division is finally transformed into 'tongues' that each can understand in their own language, although they have so many different languages. At that moment, because of the cross and resurrection, there is the possibility of a world healed of its deep and damaging wound: sin, the attempt to thwart love. The fact that language becomes so significant in Acts 2 is a recalling of the Genesis creation account, the dissolution of language at Babel, and the pointing to the history where sin is overturned, where the story of our real existence is finally told, enacted and shared. I presume that is why some onlookers thought these people were drunk: 'They have had too much wine.' People are hearing the same language event – one group thinks this signifies drunks having a party. Another group 'asked one another, "What does this mean?"', and Peter in his speech tells them that a new order has begun: 'I will pour out my Spirit on all people. Your sons and daughters will prophesy, your young men will see visions, your old men will dream dreams.' He might have added: and some will write poems. They were ecstatic, like the audiences at Allen Ginsberg's poetry readings in San Francisco. Language was taking them into new and creative relationships, although amongst Ginsberg's audiences, drugs perhaps played a part in their ecstasy!

The event between the collapse of the tower of Babel and the Spirit coming upon the chaos in Jerusalem is of course the event of Jesus Christ, his cross and resurrection. In the cross, language speaks the definitive speech act: 'Father, forgive them for they know not what they do.' And what do they do? They silence Jesus, they stop him from teaching and preaching and acting as he did. They stop him from creating his poems about a new creation so that people should not see and act anew. They. We. Then. Now. When his mute and mangled body hangs dead on the cross there is a cry from the elements of earth: darkness hovers over the earth; an earthquake shakes its foundations. I do not think it impatience or an inability to stay with suffering and loss that made the early church begin to understand the meaning of the three days between the death and resurrection. When the Word is silent and even 'absent' it is 'present'. Between death and resurrection there is a preaching by that same Word in the underworld to the souls who have waited upon this hour. This cosmic event is called 'the descent into hell' (see Pitstick, 2007 for the complexity of this doctrine). This is poignant, because Jesus' silence becomes redemptive speech. Regardless of what you as a reader might make of this mysterious tradition, it is actually part of the Apostles' Creed. As a Christian one has to make something of it. It is a very early tradition about speech acts continuing into the heart of death, precisely because death no longer has the last word.

Narrating Poems

I realise that the above requires my poems to be a miracle to the reader. This is a rather tall order, especially as they are a miracle to me only in the sense that I managed to rework them enough for them to be included here. I've started with two poems devoted to Vermeer of Delft, who is on most days, my favourite artist. I am trying to write a poem for every Vermeer picture that has safe attribution – and will also include two of the famous forgeries by Han van Meegeren (Wynne, 2006). What makes Vermeer so great? You need to stare at a painting of his rather than read my prose at this point. Look at his attention to detail, his painstaking rendering of what is to be seen within the surface of the visible, rather than behind that surface, and the sense of bathing the everyday in a light that makes it utterly absorbing and awesome. It is like the leaves in the park: a miracle because we look on at the ordinary and realise that it is far from the ordinary. It may have been Vermeer's Christian faith, first Protestant and later Roman Catholic (so that he could marry), that made him so sensual and symbolic and so sensitive to the everyday as the location of some radiant mystery (Arasse, 1994). This mystery, this more, lies within the folds of dresses bathed in sunlight, the rapt concentration on a letter being read by a woman in blue, the bolt of light catching a pearl earring that glistens like the moist lips of the young girl who has suddenly turned towards us, the crumbs of bread on the table and a slow flowing river of milk from a jug. After a long artistic history in which religious subjects are the main focus of art, Vermeer stands at a crucial turning point when religious scenes, aristocrats, noble families, and ancient myths are dispelled. Enter the human, the humdrum, the ordinary. The 'secular' emerged into art in all its remarkable beauty.

One trajectory this secularism followed was a flattening of the landscape so that art eventually became pure aesthetics without the good and true being present. In my view Piet Mondrian's late work exemplifies this. Mark Rothko represents the porous line where the modern begins again to yearn for and embrace the divine. The other trajectory is represented by Vermeer where the ordinary becomes the site of the extraordinary. Some might not agree. However, I believe that the great genius of his work is that it is precisely the secular that is the mediator of something far greater than itself. Vermeer's paintings are not unlike a sacrament: the visible mediating the invisible. His art is like poetry: it seduces you into seeing a miracle. In these two poems I've tried to evoke one artistic form to pay tribute to another (and much greater) form. I've chosen these two because my writing and reading are a constant interplay between the amorphous realms of the sacred and secular. Human relations are central to *The Concert* and a type of meditative discipline is central to *The Milkmaid*. Please google the pictures before reading these two poems or certainly after you have read them, even if you are familiar with the pictures. Or better still go to Amsterdam to see *The Milkmaid*. *The Concert* was stolen from the Isabella Steward Gardner Museum in Boston and is still missing.

The secularism of the Eucharistic echoes of *The Milkmaid* is important for it raises the question about the sacred's transformation of the secular and not only of the secular's transformation into the sacred. I explore this movement in the poem immediately following 'The Milkmaid', 'Eucharistic Anamnesis'. The Eucharist is important to me as I've narrated above, even though I sometimes find Mass quite boring. It is particularly easy for this to happen when being passive after a week of endless working. But the Eucharist demands everything in terms of attention if it is to be anything. And then that everything falls into shadow. The Eucharist is also all about life and death and the constructing of new worlds in vision and practice. The poems that follow relate to these themes where again the secular/sacred boundary is dissolved to give some glimpse of a divine reality that lies in the heart of everything, including that which seems to be its ultimate questioner: death. Thus, there are five poems dealing with death: of an imaginary woman with cancer whose friend runs a marathon in memory of her (Bristol is full of running events); a real woman, my wife Beryl, who nearly died of cancer (and I'm extremely happy she did not); a real father-in-law, Gareth Gladstone, and a real father, Francis D'Costa. My dad died while writing this chapter. Gareth's was the first death that I had sat through and it was a very great privilege. I missed my father's last breath by three hours as he lived in London and I in Bristol, but had the privilege of sitting with him, my mum and my sister for some hours together in a room provided by Central Middlesex Accident and Emergency. Death, though, seems to be one moment in life, and can become a skewed focus. One theologian calls this fascination with death necrophilia (Jantzen, 2004, 1–45). I think she is half right, but both Freud and the cross would be redundant if she were totally correct. The final poem in this section is one which celebrates the complex mimicry of monasticism in the quiet zone of a railway carriage.

I then turn to some explicitly 'religious landscapes'. There is something difficult but also very challenging in using the materials of biblical stories to create poems. They themselves are remarkable poems in opening up a strange new world to us, but picking up a detail and making it more central than in the original can bring something out that was not always so clear (or not even there perhaps?). 'The Shadow of the Holy Innocents' is a reminder to me that Christians should never be triumphalist as the magnificent truth of the gospel is always framed in thin, beautiful, delicate ice. Claims to truth have always been used to kill others and Christianity, uniquely at its centre, speaks of one who is killed. Suffering, death and tragedy mark life too deeply to be triumphalist, but at the same time, the resurrection cannot be hidden from view. But the resurrection is only authentic when the trace of blood is not denied, the suffering not glossed over, and the wound always has a scar, even when fully healed. 'I bring thee myrrh' was written as a meditation on the beautiful handcrafted statue that is part of a crib scene that is set up in Clifton Cathedral, Bristol, every year. In the baby's vulnerability we find a moment of rest and joy, even though that baby is marked for tragic death. The journey to the babe tells about journeys that we all make in life. 'The cross' that follows these two is about the complexity of very simple religious images: what they tell and what they do not. The cross without a body and with a body nailed on it are so potently different, each crying out for the other and each unable to say it all fully in one single image. The gender of the body on the cross also tells a story about all gendered bodies. The final poem here is one that links the biblical story of the flight into Egypt with contemporary flight narratives.

The next three poems extend the cultural horizon, all written in Japan on a very memorable visit to a Roman Catholic theological meeting about interfaith dialogue. My visit to a wonderful Zen Buddhist monastery was one high point and my visit to Nagasaki was a sobering high point. And Japanese food, especially sushi, was food and art in perfect balance. Japan was a kind of pilgrimage, as was a visit to Florida to see a pen-friend, Mandingo, on death row. Death row is where we all live. Mandingo is the first to say this. But some live in these torture chambers more explicitly where respectable but insane institutional violence is part of American legislation, at least in the majority of states, not unlike first-century Palestine. My friend's Muslim faith was a wonderful miracle in the midst of the hell of Florida's death row and a testimony, perhaps, that the greatest art is a human life, even when destined to be executed.

Finally, walking the costal footpath in Cornwall near Trebarwith where Beryl, Sachin and Roshan and I go as a family every year is a ritual of which I shall never get bored. Nature's sacrament is so near to all of us. There is a parallel to how we react to Christ's sacrament: be awed at it and it is a wonder; or try and control it for our own ends alone and we are doomed. Pentecost or Babel? More likely, something somewhere in between; where making nothing happen is moving the world into a different frame.

The Concert

(Johannes Vermeer, c. 1665–66)

Framed nature, tame upon the wall,
light pink skies, the early evening falls.
Trees swell and push, deep within the earth,
life giving gifts, given without mirth.

Framed nature bursts, laughing on the wall.
An evening serenade, due payment called,
swells of busty breath, colours heated hot,
the enjoyment of a joy, that is not.

Three framed around, a third pictured scene,
nature plucked taut, echoes in between.
The mirrored woman calls, score held in hand,
what does she sing to the shape of a man?

The Milkmaid

(Johannes Vermeer, c. 1568–60)

The gentle strength of forearms, one hand
cupped along the base, the other
in embrace; the pitcher yields its secret
to another, light-kissed rim.

Carnival bread, speckled with seeded sun,
lies silent, pregnant form, withholding
taste, but a banquet to the eye,
an aria to the wall.

Three nails driven into plaster, promise more.
The pocked-marked wall testifies neglect,
loss, but in such lack the light does play,
teasing texture, tone and toil.

A wicker basket, golden soiled and worn,
demands the same attention its tired weaver
gave; an act of grace and skill, intricacy
formed out of earth and sweat, hangs still.

The cloth upon the altar, thick and floured,
royal blue with crumbs, her priestly apron,
the chalice firmly placed. A sigh
upon her brow; the consecration of tedium,
or graced attention?

Eucharistic Anamnesis

Standing in communion queue
gazing at a flaking aged head,
with dank, dark checked suit.
At my right, a perfumed lass
with rings galore and lips aflame.
In front of her, stiff permed hair,
atop a tired pleated skirt.
I limp, one of the living dead.
Catholics on the move.

I sense a crumb of toast
lodged firmly as a rock against
the mouth of my pre-molar's cave.
My tongue, a grave digger's spade,
works furiously near the gates of hell.
Could the site of His visit
be shared with toast, the taste of egg,
and growing guilt?

I raise my hands to receive Him
absorbed at my power
to hold God in a sweaty palm.
In this giving, my lack disclosed.
No fast, no preparation,
but a hurried car chase,
swearing at the old maid's Jag.
My broken tailgate wiper
failed to yield a clear view.

Race for life

Women struggle up the mossy path,
moist, numbered, with pumping hearts.
One, with light butterfly wings, flapping time
to the rhyme of pain dancing in her sole.
She runs for life, a cherished friend in mind.
Sal's memory drives her jelly thighs
to stomp and rage upon the sodden earth,
that holds and eats Sal's wasted birth.

She trained for months in long loose shirts
deftly worn to beat those smirks
from men who walked their dogs at night:
'Give it your best darling'.
She didn't turn to see his face,
but heard his dog bark loud, excited by the chase.
Her daughter counted butties that she ate,
'Mum', she yawned, 'you gotta watch your weight.'

She runs for life, coated in her sweat, anxious
that her flesh is host to cells whose run for life
lives off hers; wondering if the money she collects
will build a wall to keep this death away. It won't
bring Sal up from the churning ooze.
She runs and runs. She runs for life.

The word

Medical books grow on our shelves
forming new words we master to
keep away an old familiar word.

Life punctuated by hospital visits,
post mortems on consultants words, even
gestures. Avoiding the odour of decay.

Telephone conversations: Chinese whispers,
changing words and intonations,
mantras concealing the single word

that marks an end.

For my father-in-law

There is nothing like the stillness
that hangs in the air when death
kisses and breathes the body's life.
The crickets sing, the fridge's snake rattles,
floorboards stretching in the sun, carry on
as if he was here, when he is not.

The garden's summer beauty, full scented,
blazes bright, boasting sap's profusion,
when inside, soft nettled face
and compost breath subsides. And stops.
Then starts again,
refusing any but life's own time.

The gasps of decomposing speech,
petals rustling in the wind
from the darkness seen behind
phlegm-filled eyes, drained of spring-tide.
This leaving is an age, not a minute fast.
His turkey neck twitches. Then stops.
Then starts again.

The nurse requests permission on her mobile
to push angelic dreams and stupor through his veins,
to quell the groans, the muted struggle to bloom,
who knows where. But bloom you will. And after,
sitting in the sun beating hot against my skin,
I think of yours, ancient parchment, hardly read.

10.33 to Paddington

Just as when Icarus fell, so on my train journey:
people ring friends and laugh, and near Reading,
farmers drive their tractors through sodden fields
taking hay to animals where grass is now mud,
and oozing earth joins rivers of sky.
The conductor, a joyful man, turns ticket collection
into a symphony of pleasure, kindly wishing me 'a nice day'
while your corpse grows colder at Central Middlesex A&E.
The workmen on the rails move in eerily green jackets
and the girl playing games on her mobile is transfixed.
I sit here, writing in the empty pages of 'Behold the Pierced One',
the book I quickly chose as I rushed to your death train;
the book not read, but now well written in.
Did I see you fall, head down, broken lead?

The body

Your mouth lay open with yellowing skin
and sitting near you, I could smell
the sweat from your scalp, five hours old,
a kind of familiar taste when kissing you bye
while you lay asleep or half awake.
But a sleep like this, never before.

I stroke the stubble of your head
and cradle your face, actions not familiar,
but welcomed by your quietness. Gestures
from childhood returned: touching your hands
and playing you like a piano, feeling the dying
warmth in your toes and your shoulder.

A small reptile tongue, yellow pink,
sits still, poised, as if to speak or sing,
and the hairs of your nose frozen like grasses
in a cave of dark stillness where the air
no longer moves, nor swirls or howls,
but keeps a silent vigil watching.

Can such stillness watch; or only be watched?

And your jaws with the growth of a half-day,
uneven small razor nicks streak your cheek,
threatening to bleed and not to stop.

In you, the drugs that thinned your blood
sit, tired of working, slowly being defeated.
Where is that blood? The wounds are open.

And you are still, perfectly still,
even when I try and push your jaw so that
the dark cavern of your mouth might close.

But now, there can be no change. No movement,
except decay, apart from the drugs
that will freeze your death, now just five hours old.

Quiet Zone

Despite the window stickers:
a red slash across speakers,
warning all this is the zone
of modernity's monastic space.
A young woman takes a call.
Since Darlington a peace has
reigned, unparalleled in
so many a journey; a pre-lapsarian
silence hung in carriage F.

She speaks to a baby sitter
who has failed her. She's panicked
in her calm. She speaks urgently
to a friend seeking cover.
She cannot return in time.
Her child will have no home,
no food. She will be jailed.
All unsaid.
But her calm is growing paler.
No one, four calls later, can cover.

A woman, middle-aged,
with a marriage ring, breaks
the tension between calls.
'Who do you bloody think you are?
Call after call? I got a ticket
to read in this carriage.
Behave yourself, can't you?'
Did she have children?

The silence changes tone.
The fall from the peace zone.
What of the tears of the child
who stands adrift after school?
What of her loneliness?
The mother sits
silent in the quiet zone
staring through the pane.
Such is the fragile peace
of monasteries, old and new.

The Shadow of the Holy Innocents

Did Gabriel realise that he initiated a blood bath?
Had this sublime angel missed Jeremiah's prophecy,
that Rachel's weeping in Ramah would turn into
a wailing that would never stop, not even to welcome
angels in that dung-rich Bethlehem stable?

She was highly favoured. But what of those mothers
whose sons were forced from their arms,
torn from their feeding breasts,
heads smashed on paving stones brought from Jerusalem?
Had they given a stifled *fiat*, assenting as handmaidens?

Perhaps, when Mary was disturbed by Gabriel's words,
she saw what havoc she unwittingly allowed:
giving birth to a childless son, who would unleash
such pain upon her, for she must witness
what the other mothers saw: blood on wood.

She paused, asked the question, distracting herself
from the terrifyingly obvious: her life would never be
the same, her body not her own. She would walk
in the shadow of the presence, dimly clear,
and the wailing would not cease, growing louder and near.

While nothing is impossible to God, stopping the tears
will be. These women will weep until the end of time,
spitting phlegm into the darkness of divinity that offers no solace
but remains hanging there with us. A handmaiden's lot?
'Be it done according to thy Word'.

I bring thee myrrh

You know how the stars dance their magic in the skies,
while the tent flaps rustle to the light of fireflies.
The camels breathe restless, no longer the heavens tame,
the canopy of black speckled night rent by comet flame.
We must follow the bright, even to the ends of the earth,
for our lives will begin there, where death will give birth.

At Herod's palace, our Persian carpets were treasured,
we supped on spiced plums, quail, wines without measure.
He too had sensed the earth tremble, a quickening of heart,
he too had consulted his ensemble, making the laws their art.
We all sought what would move the world on a new axis,
the coming of a power that would change our every practice.

He whispered of a small hill town, 'the House of Flesh',
Beit Lehem, and so we journeyed, dined and refreshed,
into the heat, where scorpions play on the stones and snakes
slide into shade, escaping the bread that the sun will bake
deep in the womb of the earth, where only darkness once was
and now a quickening of life, the overturning of law.

We did not believe the squalor, the damp, the smell of dung,
The straw meant only for rough cattle's tongue.
I was dressed in my best: cadmium and alizarin robes,
hot Egyptian beaten gold hung from my lobes.
Softest cured calf leather clad my feet. In my arms,
from the largest bull in Asia, a horn of ruler's balm.
Then I stopped. And you see me as I saw him then:

With an old and tired man whose eyes were wild,
with a girl lying faint, young enough to be his child
and a babe on straw upon splintered hewn wood.
He made us stare. He made us stop, just where we stood.
He was naked, though covered with his mother's love,
his father's trust and awe in the starry skies above.

This warm wet child and straggly minders all
called us near to the edge, into the fall, to gaze
and see the world anew. Look with your heart,
into the darkening light, with love ablaze.

The cross

This cross, emptied of flesh
stands mute, triumphant,
revealing soft polished wood;
not splinters, rough grain, raw-sap smell.
No burnt sienna, congealed blood
matted, discolouring the dead wood.

Linseed replaces the sour sweat scourge.
The trial of our existence, planed,
sanded, erased with human crafting.
Smell the blood of monthly woman
and see there, in misconception,
the body that hangs cursed.

Flight into England

His black skin bleached in neon light,
his wife, thin as a needle, feeds the child.
Immigrants from Sudan are trouble.
They all have incredible stories,
that make you weep in sorrow,
or in mirth. Deserts breed fantasy.

Plastic chairs hold them in position
awaiting the U.K. Border Agency.
Since she has a baby, a woman officer
is also there to comply with laws
that govern justice and drops of mercy.
The baby worries the milk-dry breast.

'Why did you leave your country?'
'Why bring your wife and child here?'
Questions worn thin from use.
Three for the price of one, includes
a cradle snatcher. He so so old
and she's a teen with an eating disorder.

The child sniffles, cries, gets pushed
back upon the nipple. The officer smiles.
The old man speaks in broken words
that fall upon the table: 'An angel spoke me.
To leave. To fly England. Was not here.'
His eyes are moist as if it hovered near.

'An angel? In your dreams?'
This was a story he had not heard.
They swapped stories and this
was new: black angels.
'Do they tell you what to do all the time?'
Perhaps the medics should be called.

The ebony man looked lost. He leant
and touched his son, gently, on the head.
'They die children' he croaked.
'Are you claiming your family's in danger?'
A category, at last, that meant something,
somewhere to pass them, a box ticked.

Nagasaki Atomic Bomb Museum: the tile exhibit

You must pay to enter history,
then slowly place your finger
on a roof tile. Let it linger.

Let it feel the scorch of heat,
half the tile, bubbled red,
scratched, ashen-dead.

This tile once saved a family
from the cold relentless rain.
Now it only lets in pain.

Zen Buddhist Temple Visit

I did not see a Buddhist monk sit,
and breathe the subtle form
of trees, the patterned stones and
fashioned moss.

Instead, a Catholic priest, cracked by love
led me by the hand to see
a glimpse of his beloved Zen,
a space of grace, in between.

Sushi

I once ate a painting,
bright colours on fine pale silk,
crafted deftly, with grace,
cultured practice,
and rolling sea.

Pilgrimage across the sea

Arrival:
A dull red orb burns the morning mist
on Holy Saturday. Nature will not mourn.
Women line up, few men, dressed for heat, to see
'ordinary population' or 'death row'. Indistinguishable
in their smoking, shuffling, and see-through bags.
She with anger at the wait, to watch death creep
through veins she once held. And guards,
catching their shift, schooled in their arts,
bark and bask before they enter.
This could be a shopping mall, a queue, waiting
for the sale, or a lynch mob in the making, marked
with anticipation, seeking out flesh.

Entrance:
Finger prints, photographs, paperwork, body search,
Counting rings, bracelets, a catalogue
of captured identity, while below the skin,
fear seeps free as another door and another door
and another, closes. Controlled from afar, so that flesh
now runs through wires, static crackling. A walk
in the morning sun, the 'dog run', metallically clean, past
mental bins, each with their own exercise cage.
Then, like a city council office it stands, alone:
death row. The windows, like sunglasses, refuse light.

The site:
More doors, then finally, three rows of sixteen tables
spawning steel spider leg seats, empty altars to hold
the banquet from the cafeteria aided by microwaves.
Furniture to aid six hours shared with a room full of killers.
Or innocents, or near insane. And him. This room will
be a suburb diner: warm greetings, guzzled food, loved ones
re-united, bored folks sharing dullness, all aware of closing time,
for the end must come, is always near.
One by one they enter, like stars on Palm Beach:
white pants and shoes, orange shirts, well cut hair.
Some sport death in their eyes, tired and drawn.
Florida's most dangerous, while alligators roam free
and sharks swim the sea.

Presence:
Four days of six-hour visits begin. A friendship of such intensity,
shared with wife, daughter, and stranger. Mandingo's life is a
gangster movie: black, poor, drug addicted mum, gangs dealing
death and crack, Darwinian dreams, and a daughter,
before being framed for a murder he did not commit. But flesh breaks
cliché, begs questions, opens up the mystery of his being. Hardly
innocent, but still on his cross. Mandingo enters my world:
a love of scripture, learning, and humour, an inner life more
vigorous than a frenzied car chase. A black broken body,
a roguish smile, a faint smell of iron in his mouth, with peach lips
and gratitude that burns away my fear. It is he, not I, who has travelled.

Absence:
After the visit, I lie floating, facing the dying sun in our motel swimming pool,
staring into blue sky with trails of glory from flights, men freely moving
over earth, etching their mark for all to see, sipping scotch and eating nuts,
in first class and economy, discreetly hiding death sentences from each other.
Here on the ground, and below, darkness sets in. Erasing trails.

The same path

Every day we took the same path
up into the open field overlooking sea,
cliffs, derelict pill-boxes braided in ivy,
used by sheep unconcerned with Huns.

Every day this same path was different,
not in toll on calf and foot, but in awe,
birthed by the sheer implacability of earth,
sea and sky dancing their fated jig.

The path robbed boredom of its victory,
won in endless flights to far off places.
But here, the planes are shooting stars
or pebbles hurled off the cliff into oblivion.

At dark, returning on the same path,
our dog inhales evening earth, breaking bracken,
scurrying into speared gorse, tongue torn from
some stray barb as if he never knew this path.

References

Arasse, Daniel, *Vermeer: Faith in Painting*, trans. Terry Grabar. (Princeton, NJ: Princeton University Press, 1994)

D'Costa, Gavin, 'The 12 Days' (5 January 2012) available at http://www.cliftondiocese.com/The-12-Days12, Accessed 27 December 2012

Eliot, T.S., *Collected poems: 1909–62* (London: Faber & Faber, 1963)

'*Genesis: Chapter 1*', Catholic Online available at http://www.catholic.org/bible/book.php Accessed 27 December 2012

Hopkins, Gerard Manley, *The Poems of Gerard Manley Hopkins* (London: Oxford University Press, 1967)

Jantzen, Grace M., *Foundations of Violence* (London: Routledge, 2004)

Keats, John, *John Keats: The Complete Poems* (London and New York: Longman Group, 1970)

Larkin, Philip, *Collected poems: 1938–1983* (London: Marvell and Faber & Faber, 1990)

Pitstick, Alyssa Lyra, *Light in Darkness: Hans Urs von Balthasar and the Catholic Doctrine of Christ's Descent into Hell* (Grand Rapids, MI: W.B. Eerdmans, 2007)

Shakespeare, William, *Hamlet* (London: Macmillan, 1891)

Steiner, George, *Real Presences* (London: Faber, 1989)

Unknown Author, 'Miracle' (July 2012) available at http://en.wikipedia.org/wiki/Miracle Accessed 27 December 2012

Williams, William Carlos, *Selected Poems* (London: Penguin Books, 1976)

Wordsworth, William, 'Preface to the Lyrical Ballads', 1800. Available at http://www.bartleby.com/39/36.html Accessed 27 December 2012

Wynne, Frank, *I was Vermeer: The Forger who Swindled the Nazis* (London: Bloomsbury, 2006)

Index